Transcripts Made Easy

The Homeschooler's Guide to High School Paperwork

Janice Campbell

Everyday Education
Making Time for Things That Matter

Edition: 3 © 2007 by Janice Campbell; 2010 by Everyday Education, LLC

Everyday Education, LLC

P.O. Box 549

Ashland, VA 23005

www.Everyday-Education.com

www.TranscriptsMadeEasy.com

Campbell, Janice

Transcripts made easy: the homeschooler's guide to high school paperwork / Janice Campbell

ISBN-10: 0-9774685-3-4

ISBN-13: 978-0-9774685-6-0

1. Education—Home Schooling. 2. Education—Reference. 3. Reference—Handbooks & Manuals. I. Title.

Standard Legal Disclaimer

The information in this book is intended to provide general record-keeping and transcript information for homeschool parents, and does not constitute legal advice or supersede the laws of your state. Because homeschool laws change fairly often, it's important to keep up with applicable regulations, and to comply with them.

The integrity of the upright shall guide them...

Proverbs 11:3a

Contents

Introduction to the Third Edition

Dear Friends,

It's time to think about high school! I hope you're excited about that, because it's one of the most interesting stages of homeschooling. There are so many wonderful things you can do with your teen. From choosing to get a jump start on college to exploring potential careers through a microbusiness, a world of possibilities is waiting for you.

However you decide to do high school, you'll need to keep records. Even if you are a relaxed homeschooler or an unschooler, you'll probably find that your student will eventually need a transcript. I'm pretty sure that you want to spend your time on the things that matter, though, rather than on heavy-duty paperwork.

That's where *Transcripts Made Easy* can help. It's a complete system that will help you plan and track your teen's classes and activities and record them in a way that showcases his or her achievements. You can pick and choose just how you want to use the system, and you can use as much or as little of it as you please. You won't even have to buy or learn to use special software!

I believe that *Transcripts Made Easy* is the most simple, streamlined method of high-school planning and record-keeping that you'll find anywhere. Hundreds of people who have used earlier editions have helped me make it that way by letting me know how they used it and asking good questions.

That's what makes this third edition special — I've included new chapters answering the questions I've most frequently heard over the past few years. I've even gotten input from real, live college counselors on what they expect to see on homeschool transcripts! In addition, I've added a new chapter featuring an interview with special-needs consultant Judith Munday on creating transcripts for special-needs students. And when you're ready to figure a grade point average for your student's transcript, just visit www.freegpacalc. com for quick and easy calculations!

Whatever your situation, whether you're following a traditional high-school course of study or are doing unusual and exciting things, you'll find what you need to know about record-keeping and transcripts in these pages. If you have a question that you don't see addressed, please e-mail me at jceved@comcast.net I'll do my best to help!

I wish you a joyous high-school experience.

Janice Campbell

Ashland, Virginia, 2007; 2010

Where To Start

Transcripts Made Easy is designed so that you can jump in at any point and use only the parts you need. Here are some suggestions to help you decide where to start.

If Your Student is in Junior High School

You're in the right place! Read through this book; choose the ideas that best suit your teaching style, and begin keeping records with the first high-school-level class your student takes. It's that easy!

If Your Student is in the First Two Years of High School

You probably already know what you're doing for academics, so just skim through the introduction to high school, and jump into the record-keeping ideas. If you haven't been keeping records, start to catch up now. If you have records of some sort, start a transcript form, and fill in as many semesters as you have completed. For the rest of high school, you may decide to use the Subject Worksheets or just continue with what you've been using. Either way, if you keep the transcript current by filling in each semester as you complete it, you can relax and know that you've got the paperwork under control!

If Your Student is a Junior

This is college application time! If you have kept records of any kind, it's time to start a transcript: choose a transcript format, set it up on your computer, and start filling it in. If you don't have many records, you can jog your memory by using the Check-Off Transcript form to remind you of the basic subject categories you need to fill in, or you may just want to start using Subject Worksheets to organize what you can remember.

If Your Student is a Senior

You may feel that you're way too late to get going, but don't worry; you can do it! You'll follow the same procedure as the parent of a junior—you'll just have to work faster!

If You Need a Transcript Tomorrow

You don't have time to worry about details! Go directly to the Check-Off Transcript and fill in the Basic Information and Identity sections. Check off each subject your student has completed. Add as many grades as possible—grades from outside sources, grades based on AP or CLEP exams, and grades you remember. If you have grades for all classes, you can follow the instructions in the How to Grade and Grant Credit chapter, but if you have grades for only some classes, include those you have and just check off classes with no grades. The college admissions department will at least see the scope of what your student has covered and will be able to evaluate his abilities through standardized test scores.

Creating the High-School Record Notebook

You'll need just a few things to create a very efficient record-keeping system for high school:

- A three-ring binder
- A copy of each of the Subject Worksheet pages
- Copies of the Reading and Activity logs
- Copies of the Class Profile sheets if you choose to use them

Where to Start

Once you have determined which forms you will need, create them using the instructions I've provided or photocopy them from the Reproducible Forms section, and place them in a three-ring binder. This "High-School Record Notebook" will serve as the central gathering place for your student's high-school records, and the filled-out forms you include will be all the supporting documentation you need to create the student's transcript.

Remember—all the forms in *Transcripts Made Easy* are here for your convenience. You don't need to use them all, just the ones that fit your situation. Record-keeping should be simple, so that you can spend time with people rather than paperwork!

To accomplish great things we must first dream,

then visualize, then plan...

Alfred A. Montapert

Nothing in life is to be feared. It is

only to be understood.

Marie Curie

Knowing your destination is half the journey.

Unknown

Introduction to High School

What is the purpose of high school? How does it differ from the eight years of school you've already completed with your student? Just as teenagers are different from toddlers, high school is different from the years that have gone before. There are several areas of change:

- Level of difficulty in school subjects
- Level of student independence
- Increased options for outside study
- Increased responsibility for keeping records

Of the four major changes, the record-keeping responsibility may be the one that is keeping you awake at night. Help for difficult subjects can be found in many places, but record-keeping is a responsibility that tends to fall most heavily on the teaching parent!

Many states require very little in the way of record-keeping, so high school may be the first time you have had to think about it. If this is the case, don't worry—*Transcripts Made Easy* offers everything you need to minimize the time you spend on paperwork. This will help you make time for things that matter—including helping your teen take advantage of the many academic opportunities available to nontraditional students.

Planning to Make the Most of High School

There are several factors to consider as you plan your student's high-school education. An ideal education not only sparks a lifelong interest in study, but also

- Fits the student's aptitudes, interests, and goals
- Prepares the student for life as an adult
- Becomes increasingly self-directed
- Meets or exceeds the requirements of law
- Meets or exceeds the requirements for entrance to the college or vocation of the student's choice
- Provides opportunity to acquire practical skills

The primary thing I'd like you to notice about this list is the focus on the student—the education experience should be personalized to fit his or her needs, talents, and goals. This means that high school will probably be different for each of your children. (I'm sorry! I know that one-size-fits-all may seem easier than custom-made, but one of the beauties of homeschooling is the ability to respond to our children as individuals rather than as cogs in a vast machine.) Some students will enjoy being part of the planning process, but most seem content to let Mom do it.

Some students will have clear interests and be easy to plan for, while others will want to opt for a more generic course of study. No matter how many children you have, you can rest assured you will probably end up creating that many different high-school plans! I planned a history-centered high-school experience that delighted my oldest son, and was quite surprised when I had to design something entirely different for my second son, who was deeply interested in computer programming. My third and fourth sons have also chosen different paths based upon their interests, so with four boys, I ended up creating four different high-school experiences.

The Can't-Miss Basics

High school looks a lot less intimidating when you realize that your college-bound student needs only sixteen core credits (also known as Carnegie units) and eight elective credits, for twenty-four total units. Students who are not college bound need even less—twenty-two credits—thirteen core credits and nine elective credits. A two-semester class earns one Carnegie unit, so the twenty-four-credit requirement can be broken down to four years of high school, six classes per year. That's not too bad, is it?

I recommend that students take at least one year of a foreign language, even if they are not college bound. It is helpful not only in understanding the structure of English but also in the work world, where bilingual workers are increasingly needed. Below are a few other recommendations from my book *Get a Jump Start on College! A Practical Guide for Teens*. These are the essential skills your student will need to succeed in both high school and college.

Essay and Research Report Writing

Your student needs excellent composition skills, practice in both timed and untimed essay and report writing, and an understanding of the most commonly used methods of citation, as outlined below. A basic handbook such as *Write for College* (by Patrick Sebranek, et al.) provides instructions for researching, writing, revising, and proofreading various types of essays, as well as help in developing the skills listed as Writing Basics.

Writing Basics Your Student Needs to Know
- The five-paragraph essay
- The Five-Step Writing Process:
  1. Read/Research
  2. Think on Paper (brainstorming)
  3. Organize Ideas
  4. Write
  5. Revise
- How to use writing handbooks and research materials

Citations

I recommend your student learn the following citation methods that are required for various types of classes:

- MLA (Modern Language Association): This method of in-text citations seems to be most often used in literature and other humanities classes. I find it the most simple and logical method of citation, and it seems to be growing in popularity.

- APA (American Psychological Association): Another method of in-text citation that is usually required in the social sciences.

- *Chicago Manual of Style*: This is a citation system, using footnotes and endnotes, that is often used in history and humanities classes.

Online Research

This is an essential component of any education. Your student must learn to conduct specific searches, select credible sources, and correctly cite information used. Online research can save astonishing amounts of time and money, but, like traditional research, can be done badly. Research can seem easy with the Internet, but he or she must still check facts and avoid plagiarism. Never just cut and paste from the information found online!

Credible Research Resources
- Databases offered through the local or college library
- Encyclopedia sites (though information is usually very general)
- Sites hosted by colleges (URL ends in .edu)

Personal Organization

You would find it helpful to keep a three-ring binder for each subject your student studies and each class he or she takes. Into it put the class syllabus and schedule, plus copies of all notes and written assignments. That way, everything related to the subject stays together and is organized for easy review. I like to use plastic sheet protectors so that I don't have to punch holes in every sheet of paper.

Time Management

If your student is old enough to do college-level work, he is old enough to plan his time wisely. He must learn to look at project due dates and create intermediate deadlines for each step of a project. Careful planning can prevent last minute cramming for a test or turning in an inferior essay because he didn't start soon enough.

If he needs to learn time-management skills, he may want to look at Sean Covey's *The 7 Habits of Highly Effective Teens* or Julie Morgenstern's *Time Management from the Inside Out.*

Test-Taking Skills

Your student should learn the techniques that will increase his chances for success on a standardized test. These include knowing how to manage time, understanding the best way to approach multiple-choice questions, having a game plan for timed essays, and understanding the scoring system for the particular test. Other books in my *Doing College Your Way* series will address these points in more detail, but he needs to be aware that these are skills he will need to learn and practice for maximum success.

Be sure that he takes one or more sample exams from a test-prep book before taking a real college-level exam. That way, he will have few surprises and will feel much more confident when taking the real thing! For the most part, I suggest using the test-prep books published by the company that publishes the actual exams. The sample problems they offer seem to be most like the questions on the tests.

Counselor Success Tips

I interviewed many college counselors as I worked on this edition of the book, and one of the questions I asked was:

What is the most important thing a student can do in high school to prepare for college-level schoolwork?

Here are some of the answers I received. Remember that each of the counselors is expressing his or her opinion, as well as describing school policy.

Rob Bovey, Corban College

"College-level schoolwork is definitely more intense then schoolwork assigned in high school! However, this should not cast fear into the heart of the aspiring high school grad. By developing good time management skills, learning to associate with others who will encourage good study habits, communicating with teachers, and when needed, utilizing academic services such a tutor or study group, students should find few troubles adjusting the new demands of college academia."

Mark Lapreziosa, Arcadia University

"Taking a rigorous course load, including courses in Math, Science, Foreign Language, English and Social Studies each year, including the senior year, is the best way to prepare for college-level schoolwork. Also, read a book a week."

Karen P. Condeni, Ohio Northern University

"Develop and sustain good study habits and time management. The level of discretionary time in college necessitates a good use of time—know when to work and when to play. Do not procrastinate; it does come back to create the last minute crisis and cramming and doesn't work well."

James Townsend, LeTourneau University

"Learn what high school courses can help prepare you for college level courses in your major. If you want to be an engineer then you're better off taking math courses instead of enjoying a semester of 'Introduction to Swedish Grammar.'"

Introduction to High School

Kelly Stoner, Wilson College

"What I feel is the most important thing a high school student should do to prepare for college level work is to know how to research properly and really comprehend what they are researching. The best way to research is to know both sides of the story before you defend a side."

Jeffrey C. Mincey, Grove City College

"The student must challenge themselves by taking the most academically demanding courses that they possibly can in order to develop superior study skills. It will not be their high GPA or their high test scores that will make them successful; instead it will be their study habits and their time management skills that will make or break them."

Kim McCarty, Seton Hill University

"Be sure you are taking a college prep curriculum. This is very important in order to prepare for college level coursework. Honors and Advanced coursework may be helpful, although not required at SHU. Service learning and experiential learning are also very important."

Jolane Rohr, Manchester College

"Take as much math as possible, and take English courses that require analytical reading and writing."

Jenni Burke, Corban College

"Learning to write well is one of the most important things a student can do to prepare for college. The ability to communicate ideas clearly is crucial to college success."

Monica Inzer, Hamilton College

"The single best predictor of success in the college classroom is success in the high school classroom. Hamilton is a challenging environment so we want to see that students have done well within the most rigorous curriculum available to them (that still allows success)."

Nancy Davidson, Augustana College

"Students who take challenging courses are better prepared. They become accustomed to the workload and the higher expectations. It is important that students balance their courseload so they have rigorous courses throughout their high school career. Those students who strive to get all of the difficult courses in prior to their senior year and then slide are doing themselves a disservice."

Sam Smith, Stonehill College

"Read as much as possible and work on effective writing. Try to take academically challenging courses in the five major academic areas. The more challenging the courses you take the more competitive the range of colleges that will consider you."

Moishe B. Singer, MPH, Yeshiva University

"Take as many advanced courses as possible to show that they can succeed in upper level courses. I am always more impressed by slightly lower grades of all honors courses than straight A's of a minimal load/normal courses."

Graduation Requirement Summary

Most states have two sets of graduation requirements for their public-school students, one for college-bound students and one for everyone else. Here is a fairly standard sample. Remember that the college of your choice may require more credits in some subject areas!

High-School Graduation Requirements	Standard Diploma (General Ed.)	Advanced Diploma (College Prep)
English	4	4
Math (All but one unit must be Algebra I or above)	3	4
Science (Earth Science, Biology, Chemistry, Physics)	3	4
History/Social Science	3	4
Foreign Language		3
Health/Physical Education	2	2
Fine Arts/Practical Arts	1	1
Electives	6	2
Total Units Needed	22	24

Resources for Determining What to Study in High School

College Catalog

If your teen has a particular college in mind, request the college catalog early during the high-school years so you can find out exactly what is required for admission. If he has no specific college in mind, any college website or catalog should provide enough information to be useful. Just keep in mind that the more selective the school, the more competitive the entrance requirements. The catalog will usually also contain information on what college-level exams are accepted for credit. Many colleges have websites where this information is posted, so you can do much of your research from your computer.

Standards of Learning Objectives

Many states have very detailed lists of learning objectives. Copies of these are usually available through your state homeschool organization or Department of Education. If you are required by your state's homeschool law to meet or exceed the SOL objectives in language arts and math, it is important to get a copy of the objectives early enough to be sure your curriculum covers all the bases.

State Requirements

Your state's Department of Education (DOE) has established basic graduation requirements for the public schools. You can use these as general guidelines for your transcript, especially if your student doesn't plan to go to college. To find out what these requirements are, go to http://education.umn.edu/nceo/TopicAreas/Graduation/StatesGrad.htm, or check your state's DOE website (search for it using Google® or another search engine).

If you don't have Internet access, you can call the DOE and request a copy. The number can be found in the government section of the phone book. You don't have to identify yourself as a homeschooler—any citizen may request a copy of the state's high-school graduation requirements.

Standardized Tests to Take

There are a number of standardized tests that may be taken in high school. While each type of exam consists primarily of multiple-choice questions, the exams are designed to measure different things. You can take exams to gain college entrance, to add credibility to your transcript grades, and to get a head start on college (see www.GetaJumpStartOnCollege.com for more information on how this works).

Aptitude Tests

The most commonly taken exams—the Preliminary Scholastic Aptitude Test (PSAT), the Scholastic Aptitude Test (SAT), and the ACT (formerly American College Testing)—measure aptitude for college-level work in language arts and math. One or more of these exams are usually required for college admissions. The PSAT, usually taken in eleventh grade, is not necessary for college admission, but taking it allows students to compete for a National Merit Scholarship.

Knowledge and Achievement Tests

A second group of exams, including the Advanced Placement (AP) and the SAT II exams, test knowledge in specific subjects in order to grant advanced placement in college. A third group of exams, which includes CLEP and DSST, tests subject knowledge in order to grant college credit. The AP and SAT II exams are administered through high schools, while the CLEP and DSST exams are administered through colleges. You can find all the details of how to register through the websites listed in the Resources chapter.

Equivalency Examination

One other exam, the General Equivalency Diploma (GED), is often taken as a substitute for a high-school diploma by people who have dropped out of high school. For this reason, I don't recommend taking it. If you have a transcript showing the required number of credits for high-school graduation, you have completed high school. The federal government, in a 1998 amendment to the Higher Education Act (HEA), allows homeschool parents to certify, in order for the student to get into the military or obtain financial aid, that their student has completed school. There is no legal requirement to take the GED in addition to completing high school.

If a college insists a student must have a GED score, they have obviously not had much experience with homeschoolers! And you have the opportunity to courteously educate them. Most colleges accept other standardized-test scores in lieu of the GED, and if one has any college credit (from college-level exams or a community college) on one's transcript, they usually don't even mention the GED. However, if you and your student run into a college that refuses to accept anything but a GED, there are two choices:

- Choose a more homeschool-friendly college.
- Take the GED, but don't record results on the transcript.

It's up to you, and the decision depends on how much your student wants to attend a particular school, and how annoyed you are by uncooperative bureaucracy!

Creative Scheduling Options

Although traditional schools follow the four-years/six-subjects-per-year formula for high school, it is certainly not carved in stone. There is no good reason why homeschoolers cannot study subjects as they please. Here are some possible alternative schedules to consider.

Sequential Scheduling

Study one subject at a time, full time. As we will discuss in "How to Grant Credit," a year of study can be measured as 120 hours or the time it takes to cover a standard textbook. A highly motivated teen could work through one textbook per month by studying about six hours a day, five days a week and could complete high school in 22 to 24 months! Alternatively, he could study two subjects at a time, three hours per day each, and finish in the same amount of time.

Clustering

Group similar subjects together so that related knowledge is gained at the same time, bolstering retention. For my sons, I grouped western civilization, British literature, art history, and music appreciation into one year, followed by a year of American history, government, and literature. Science and math can be grouped in similar ways.

College-Style Schedule

Study one group of subjects, such as math and science, on Monday and Wednesday, and the remaining subjects on Tuesday and Thursday, spending approximately two hours per day per subject. Use Friday as a study day to complete any leftover work.

High School Q&A

How early do I need to start planning?

Ideally, the junior-high school years can be used to map out a plan for high school, but you can start wherever you are. Just pull together information about what you have done so far, start filling out the worksheets, and go on from there.

What about "gaps"?

If you are starting to fill out the transcript when your student has almost completed school, you may notice that he is lacking classes in one or more of the important academic areas. You have several options, depending upon his future plans. If he is college bound, you may need to delay his graduation to complete the extra classes at home, or you may decide to enroll him in the needed subjects at the community-college level and count them as dual credit.

Does the student need an accredited diploma?

No. The diploma simply acknowledges that the student has finished high school in accordance with the laws of your state, and under a 1998 amendment to the Higher Education Act (HEA), homeschooling parents may self-certify this.

How can I teach subjects I don't remember?

Everyone worries about teaching things like higher math (if you want to see me turn pale, just break out an algebra textbook!), foreign language, and lab sciences. Fortunately, homeschooling through high school doesn't mean that you have to teach those subjects yourself. There are many ways for your student to learn a challenging subject. They can:

- Self-teach from a good textbook or video course (this works best for subjects the student enjoys).

- Take an online class. There are links to various providers from my website (www.EverydayEducation.com), and you can also use search engines to look for any type of class you need.

- Take a community college class (my favorite way to "teach" lab sciences—colleges usually have great lab equipment).

- Take the course via video or satellite school, such as Bob Jones or A Beka.

- Join a homeschool co-op that offers classes in high-school subjects.

- Find a tutor through a local college or tutoring service.

- Enroll in a distance learning high school such as Keystone, Clonlara, or Seton.

My homeschooler did high-school algebra in seventh grade. Can I count it on the transcript?

You may record all high-school work on the transcript, no matter when it was completed. Colleges are interested in *what* has been studied, not *when* it was studied. If you have a student who begins high school early and/or takes extra classes in a subject, I suggest listing the four most advanced classes in each subject area on the transcript. It's not necessary to include the date when each class was taken—just list them in the order they were completed. As you will see in the next question, you may also choose a transcript format that allows you to include all high-school-level credits.

What about too many credits?

Some homeschoolers are faced with the problem of too many credits to fit on the traditional one-page transcript. In this case, you can choose either to weed out repetitive class listings or to go with the "more is better" philosophy. The check-off format of the fourth transcript sample in the back of the book would also accommodate a very large number of credits on one page. Too many credits doesn't qualify as a problem—it's just one of the benefits of homeschooling!

"Education should have two objects: first, to give definite knowledge, reading and writing, language and mathematics, and so on; secondly, to create those mental habits which will enable people to acquire knowledge and form sound judgments for themselves." Bertrand Russell, 1872–1970

Seven Things You Can Do While You Homeschool Through High School

Build Strong Relationships

As my boys have grown through their teen years and into adulthood, it's been a joy to watch our relationship develop and change. Without negative peer influences teaching them that they shouldn't like or respect their parents, the boys have remained a delightful part of the family. It's fun to have real conversations with your young people, and to see them bring their own insights, knowledge, and understanding to the discussion.

Get a Jump Start on College

Why spend four years just doing high school, when you could exert a little extra effort and earn college credit at the same time? By taking advantage of college-level exams, community college and online classes, and other opportunities, it's possible to graduate from college when most teens are graduating from high school.

Serve Others Through Volunteering

I've heard it said that teenagers are old enough to be useful, but young enough to be dangerous. One thing that can help a teen through this awkward stage of life is serving others. There are countless volunteer opportunities, formal and informal, within the church and community. Homeschooled teens have the opportunity to learn while meeting real needs for real people.

Start a Microbusiness

What could be better than a summer job flipping burgers? Entrepreneurship, for one thing. Just think—instead of spending time in a mindless entry-level job, teens can start and run small businesses, and not only earn money for the future, but also learn about planning, budgeting, organization, marketing, and customer service, and perhaps even gain experience for a future career.

Do Career Sampling or an Apprenticeship

In traditional school, you're lucky to get one day off each year to shadow a worker at his or her job. Homeschooled teens can try different careers through informal mentoring relationships, formal apprenticeships, or volunteering opportunities.

Develop Special Talents

Have you noticed who is winning spelling and geography bees, music competitions and chess tournaments, debates and robotics competitions? Homeschooled students are often at the very top of these contests. Why? It's because they have time to pursue special interests. If they want to spend three hours a day practicing violin, there are no deadlines. They don't have to put down their instrument after 45 minutes and go rushing off to algebra or soccer.

Learn Through Travel

Just over a century ago, well-educated students were expected to complete their schooling with a Grand Tour of the world. While you may not have the resources for a Grand Tour, you can probably travel to nearby historic sites, visit other states, or, yes, even travel around the world. By preparing wisely and choosing to travel when rates are low, you can experience different cultures and make unique memories without breaking your budget. Travel can be an education all by itself!

College Admissions

One purpose for keeping good records and creating a transcript is to make it possible for your student to attend college. One of the most encouraging things I can tell you is that more and more colleges are getting excited about homeschoolers. They have found that homeschooled students are likely to be mature, self-motivated, independent learners, and their background and experiences contribute to the diversity (a magic word) of the campus. Home education is no longer a strange, lunatic-fringe movement but is an increasingly respected choice.

If you are concerned about whether or not a college is homeschool-friendly, just search their website for "homeschool" or "home school" to find what their policies are. Colleges with good homeschool policies will have the same requirements for all students, and are happy to accept a parent-created transcript as long as it contains all the standard information. As mentioned earlier, if you encounter a college that "requires" a GED or a third-party transcript (very rare), you can usually assume they have little experience with homeschoolers. You may choose to avoid the college, or you may correspond or meet with the admissions department to try to arrange a compromise.

The Paperwork Jungle

If you have been to college, it's likely that you can help your student through the required applications and testing. For those who haven't been to college, don't worry—you can find your way through the maze. The key is to stay focused and keep it simple. Remember that there are only three primary things your student will need in order to get into college:

1. A transcript

2. Required standardized tests, taken on schedule

3. Filled-out college applications (some will include essays)

That's the list! It doesn't look too intimidating, does it? I have provided a four-year plan at the end of this chapter to help you remember what to do when. If your student has chosen to accelerate high school and finish in two or three years, just drop the first year or two of the plan and follow the schedule for the final two or three years.

Be sure to review the Counselor Success Tips and Can't-Miss Basics sections in the Introduction to High School chapter as you plan each year of high school. That will help ensure you aren't leaving out any of the essential skills that will help your student succeed.

What College Counselors Want to See

What do college admissions counselors look for in an application packet? To find out, I surveyed admissions counselors across the country. It was interesting to hear what they had to say, and the most interesting thing of all was that their answers to my questions were often quite different from one another. This reinforces my belief that there is a college for everyone!

If your student chooses a college based upon how well its academic and social focus fits his interests, goals, and experiences, chances are that he is the kind of student the college is interested in recruiting, and he will have a pretty good chance of being admitted. However, if he chooses a college based simply upon its location, its reputation, or its athletic teams, he may or may not be the kind of student the college wants. If the college is seeking students with an academic profile far higher than his,

his chances of admission are slim. It pays to do enough research to find the college that best fits the student—it can help prevent disappointment and frustration both during the application process and after he starts school.

Here are my survey questions, with answers and quotes from the counselors who included comments with their survey responses and agreed to be quoted. You can find contact information for each of these counselors in the Resources chapter.

Q: Do standardized-test scores add credibility to a homeschool transcript?

A: Almost all respondents said "yes" to this question.

Sam Smith, Stonehill College

"Standardized test scores are required of all applicants whether they are in a regular high school or are being homeschooled. Standardized testing is more important for a homeschooled student than for other students because they allow us to compare the student's performance against other students. SAT II subject tests and ACT tests are probably more valuable than SAT I tests as they give us more insight to a student's preparation in specific academic areas."

Jennifer Burke, Corban College

"Standardized test scores definitely add credibility to homeschool transcripts. When we see a homeschool student with a 4.00, we look to see if they have a high SAT or ACT score to endorse the validity of their academic record."

Lois Harbison, Seton Hill University

"Although we do view the SAT/ACT scores as a criteria for acceptance, we also have a Write Option. A student that has not taken the exams may choose to do this. It requires that they send two essays, three pages or longer, that have been graded during their junior or senior year. Although we find that many of our homeschoolers take the SAT or ACT, we are pleased to offer other options for them as well as for other students."

Moishe B. Singer, Yeshiva University

"Yes, as the scores from homeschool are much harder to norm over several students."

Kelly Stoner, Wilson College

"They don't show credibility, but they do show a standard format that will help in comparison to the school district."

Q: Are you favorably or unfavorably impressed by AP or dual-credit classes and weighted grade points? Why?

A: All but one counselor indicated that they were favorably impressed by advanced coursework.

Tamara Lapman, Arcadia University

"We are favorably impressed by these classes because they show that students are challenging themselves and thereby continuing to grow both academically and intellectually."

Karen Condeni, Ohio Northern University

"I am favorably impressed as it denotes extra rigor and a commitment to academic challenges."

James Townsend, LeTourneau University

"We love to see students with AP and Dual-Credit courses. Yet we do not use weighted GPA in our scholarship decisions."

Lois Harbison, Seton Hill University

"At Seton Hill, we don't necessarily look for AP Classes. However, if a student has taken the exams and scored a 3 or higher, we give college elective credit. We view it as a bonus for the student."

Jolane Rohr, Manchester College

"Impressed. A strong curriculum is the best indicator of a student's ability to have a successful transition to college-level work."

Jennifer Burke, Corban College

"Favorably. Students who take AP classes show that they are willing to work at a higher lever than the average high school student. Not only do they benefit by receiving college credits for their work, they are more prepared for the rigors of collegiate academics."

Nancy Davidson, Augustana College

"We are impressed with AP courses and grant credit for scores of 4 and 5. Dual credit, it depends on the courses and who taught them. We are more impressed with challenging courses taken on a college level. We appreciate high schools who make the effort to weight grades. It's an incentive for students to take more challenging courses."

Moishe B. Singer, Yeshiva University

"Unfavorably—AP's are not what they used to be. They don't represent real college work. Also, we see past weighted grades. Having a score over 4.0 is bogus."

Sam Smith, Stonehill College

"We are favorably impressed by any academically challenging course work a student takes, whether the student is in a traditional high school or is being homeschooled. Some dual-credit courses are fine as they show us how a student will perform in a traditional educational environment. But we don't like to see too many dual-credit college level courses taken too early in a high school student's career—for example when they are 15 or 16. We feel it is probably in their best interest to take academically challenging courses at a local high school with students their age than in a college environment with older students. But we will evaluate everything that a student provides."

Q: What is the most important thing a student can do in high school to prepare for college-level schoolwork?

A: Most of these responses were variations on the theme of "read a lot, take challenging courses, learn to write well, and develop good study habits." The full text of these comments appears in the Introduction to High School chapter.

Four-Year Plan for College-Bound Students

	Course Plan	Test	Applications to Mail	Skills to Develop	Other
Year 1	6 classes: 1 unit of each core subject			Time Management Note-Taking	Read widely; record it in the Reading Log. Begin considering career aptitudes.
Year 2	6 classes: 1 unit of each core subject			Test-Taking	Begin researching colleges/alternatives.
Year 3	6 classes: Core subjects plus electives	Fall: PSAT Spring: SAT or ACT	May/June: Begin sending college applications.	Essay Writing: Timed and Untimed	Narrow college and career options. Visit colleges during spring break.
Year 4	6 classes: Core subjects plus electives	SAT II, AP, CLEP as required. Retake SAT/ACT if desired.	Apply for financial aid at www.FAFSA.gov, and individual scholarships as needed.	Continue to maintain all skills.	Register for scholarship search engines such as www.fastweb.com. (There are current links for more scholarship search engines at my website.

Tools For Keeping Records

The key to keeping paperwork simple is to settle on a single system and use it effectively. The forms in this book are a complete system, and I think you will find them very easy to use. The Subject Worksheets and the Class Profiles can be copied or printed out and placed into a three-ring binder (the High-School Record Notebook), and this will be all you need to create the transcript. However, if you enjoy record-keeping, there are other tools you may enjoy incorporating into your system.

Datebook

One organizing tool that bridges the gap between personal and school planning is the datebook. I currently use a 5½" x 8½" binder with week-at-a-glance pages from FranklinCovey, but any type of organizer would work. The school-related notes I enter here are brief, as my daily columns are narrow, but they serve to remind me to record the book or activity on the appropriate worksheet when I have time. I keep about three months' worth of calendar pages in the book at one time, and have tabbed dividers in the back where I can record important information. The datebook is what I take with me when I go out, while the High-School Record Notebook stays at home.

Reading Log

Since reading is arguably the single most important thing a student can do to prepare for life and improve his education, a reading log is a very useful tool. Keeping track of your student's reading can help you maintain a balanced reading program, and a well-rounded reading list can be a nice supplement to a college admission essay. It's also fun to look back at a high-school reading log and recall favorite and not-so-favorite books. I have provided a simple Reading Log form that your student can use, or he or she may choose to record reading in a journal or in a computer file. Whichever you choose, be sure it's legible!

Activities Log

If your student participates in many extracurricular activities, it is a good idea to keep track of them for the transcript. The Activities Log worksheet has space to list each activity, the date, and the amount of time involved. By keeping track of activities, you will be able to add up the time spent and know when the student has accumulated enough time to earn credit for the activity.

Be sure to record activities such as hobbies, sports, or vocational training, as well as academic activities (science fairs, debate club, and so forth), for nearly everything is worth at least some credit. Remember that public schools give credit for choir, journalism, band, independent living (formerly home economics), typing, and other classes that aren't strictly academic in nature. Learning is learning, and it's all valuable.

If you are grading retrospectively and haven't filled out the Activities Log, find out how many units your state or the college of your choice requires for each area of study. You and your student can then look at your datebooks, photo albums, or journals for activities and studies that fit into each area. It's harder to collect information retrospectively, but it can be done.

File Folders

I recommend keeping a single file pocket or folder for each student for each year of high school. It should be in a convenient place, such as a file drawer or portable file box, so that you can easily toss in great essays, drawings, test results, a class description, and other things that seem important. If it's not accessible, you will pile instead of file, even though the one-folder-per-year-per-student system is as simple as you're going to get.

You don't have to keep much, even if you plan to compile a portfolio along with the transcript. Remember, whatever you save will be part of what you end up storing for your student until he has a place of his own, so just keep a good representative sample of what he does. I use the materials in the file folders to jog my memory when thinking about grades and working on transcripts, as well as to remind me of how individual and special each of my children is.

How to Use Subject Worksheets

The Subject Worksheets are what you use to translate the student's activities and personal reading into credit-earning classes. These worksheets are also where you record all classes and exams the student completes. I have provided a worksheet for each of the primary areas of study (in the Reproducible Forms section at the back of the book). Use them to record what you plan to do, are doing, or have done, then transfer the information in concise form to your final transcript.

Each worksheet has space to record unit requirements, briefly identify and describe the course, and note test scores, awards, and special achievements. There's even space to note the number of college-level credits earned by exams or Advanced Placement classes. Once you've made notes on these sheets, filling out the actual transcript should be pretty simple!

So What Goes on the Subject Worksheets?
- Textbooks studied
- Academic contests such as debate, robotics, or Math Olympiad
- Unit-study projects completed
- Academically focused field trips
- Co-op or college classes

- AP or college-level exams

- Scouting, 4-H, and other community-based experiences

- Choir, instrumental music, missions, and other church-based activities

- Learning experiences gained through work, travel, or volunteer service

How to List Unit Studies on the Worksheets

If you use unit studies, remember that some activities may fit into more than one category, so you will probably end up with several fractions of a credit placed on different Subject Worksheets. For example, if your student spends a semester researching and writing about the kings and queens of England, you could assign a ½ credit of English or of history, or ¼ credit each. Purchased unit studies, such as KONOS's *History of the World*, usually specify exactly how much credit is earned for each of the topics covered.

Sample Subject Worksheet: What's On It, and Why

On the next page is a sample of a Subject Worksheet for an English class. You will notice there are several types of items entered on the worksheet. At the top of the worksheet, the subject is identified, and basic information, such as the number of credits needed and earned, is summarized. This is followed by the body of the worksheet, in which you see a variety of items recorded: a standard English class; a college-level exam; two one-semester, focused-subject English classes; a college class. This is the type of information you'll want to record for each subject. You don't need daily details or class-content information, as the class content will be summarized on the Class Profile sheets if you choose to use them.

Remember that high-school credits are what your student receives from you. College classes or college-level exams earn credit that is awarded by the college, not by the parent. However, those higher-level classes and exams should be included on the transcript; they add weight and credibility to a high-school transcript. (Read more about this in the Grading chapter.) Record credits earned by exam with an (E) or the exam abbreviation, such as CLEP or DANTES, after the course title on the transcript. Record classes taken from a school or college with the school's initials following the course title.

Subject Worksheet: English (Sample)

High-school units required: State __4__ College __4__ Other _____

Units earned: Grade 9 __1__ Grade 10 __1.5__ Grade 11 __1.5__ Grade 12 _____

College-level credits earned: Total __9__ By Exam _____ Class _____

Units/ Credits Earned	Description of Class, Test, or Activity	Grade	Date	Test Score	Comments
1	English 9 (Bob Jones University Press)	A	Fall-Spr. 2013		
1 unit; 6 coll. credits	Analysis and Interpretation of Literature (CLEP)	A*	Fall 2014	79/90 95th percentile	
½	Comparative Literature: Allegory, Myth, & Fantasy from Ancient to Modern Times	A	Spr. 2014		
	Writer's Digest Contest: Entered short story.				Won prize in online story contest
½	Survey of the Short Story: Norton Anthology of Short Fiction	A	Fall 2014		
	Field trip to Edgar Allen Poe museum; blog post & 3-page report.		10/16/14		
1 unit; 3 coll. Credits	English Literature to 1688 (JSRCC)	A**	Spr. 2015		

** College-level exams and classes will earn weighted grade points.

How to Use Class Profile Sheets

While the Subject Worksheets provide a place to list reading and activities as your student does them, the Class Profile sheets are designed to help you plan ahead. The information you record on them will serve as a bird's-eye view of what is covered during a semester or year. You can also keep the profiles as backup information for the transcript, if an admissions counselor happens to ask for additional documentation of what your student has done.

For subjects such as math, which don't involve instructions more detailed than "work through the even problems in the daily lesson," you really don't need to fill out a Class Profile (unless you just want a profile for every class). These worksheets are designed for classes in which there is reading from multiple sources and there are specific assignments or exams that form a basis for granting credit.

Sample Class Profile: What's On It, and Why

I have filled out a sample Class Profile, using information from the *Excellence in Literature* curriculum (*English IV: British Literature*- www.ExcellenceInLiterature. com). Notice that I include only the primary texts in the list of readings. Shorter items are listed in the curriculum as "context readings," and can be seen in detail there. In the same way, assignments are described only briefly, because complete information is easily accessible in the textbook. Remember, this profile is only a bird's-eye view— complete details aren't necessary!

Class Profile (Sample)

Class: *Excellence in Lit: English IV, British Literature*   **Date:** *Fall 2010*

Description: *This is the first semester of a two-semester course studying British Literature chronologically and in context. There is an honors option available with extra reading and a research assignment at the end of the year; we will decide whether to do this after the semester begins.*

Outside Resources/Tutors: *None*

Final Grade/Comments:

Readings	Assignments
* *Unit 1 - Middle English: Beowulf* * *Unit 2- Selections from Canterbury Tales by Geoffrey Chaucer* * *Unit 3 - Edmund Spenser, Sir Gawain and the Green Knight, and the Arthurian Legend* * *Unit 4 - King Lear by William Shakespeare* * *Unit 5 - Paradise Lost by John Milton* * *Unit 6 - Pride and Prejudice by Jane Austen* * *Unit 7 - Great Expectations by Charles Dickens* * *Unit 8 - Wuthering Heights by Emily Brontë* * *Unit 9 - To the Lighthouse by Virginia Woolf* *Context readings from Norton Anthology, library and online resources* *Poets studied include Donne, Herbert, Marvell, and many others*	*Author Profile for each unit* *1- Beowulf: Historical Approach paper; Retell as modern prose or write analytical essay* *2- Canterbury Tales: Middle English exercise; 750-word comparison essay* *3- Sir Gawain: Approach Paper; Faerie Queene: Record epigraphs; Analytical essay on 1 of 2 topics* *4- Scene summaries; Compare/contrast essay* *5- Summarize each book in the epic; Analytical essay on 1 of 2 topics* *6- Letter-writing exercise; Poetry analysis or analytical essay* *7- Approach paper & character essay* *8- Journalism exercise; Analytical essay on 1 of 2 topics* *9- Approach paper or retelling; Analytical essay on 1 of 2 topics* *Vocabulary from Classical Roots*

Grading: Course grade is based upon essays (65%), shorter assignments (15%), vocabulary (10%), and studentship (10%).

How To Do Anything

Little by little,

Bit by bit;

By the yard, it's hard,

By the inch, what a cinch!

– Encouragement from a children's song

Good plans shape good decisions.

That's why good planning

helps to make elusive dreams

come true.

– Lester R. Bittel

Naming Classes

Students who follow a traditional curriculum don't usually have much trouble naming classes. However, if you have put together your own curriculum, or if you're a relaxed homeschooler or an unschooler, one challenge you will face is translating unconventional learning experiences into official-sounding class names. Once you get going, however, you'll find that it's easy, and can almost be fun.

Basic Ideas for Naming

You can keep it totally simple by going with the traditional and obvious options. You can choose to call your classes any of the following:

- Subject plus year (English 9, 10, 11, 12)
- Subject plus a Roman numeral (History I, II, III, IV)
- Specific subject name (Biology, English Literature, Chinese History)
- Textbook name (Saxon *Algebra I,* Rosetta Stone French I)
- Publisher and subject (Memoria Press Latin, Tapestry of Grace World History, Excellence in Literature English IV: *World Literature*)

- Author and subject (Jay Wile Chemistry)
- Curriculum provider and subject (Sonlight 20th Century History, John Tyler Community College Biology I)

Getting Creative With Class Names

If you want to get creative, there are many ways you can choose to list a class or activity. For example, if your teenager has built a business in baby sitting, he or she may have taken Red Cross courses in childcare, learned about business record-keeping, and read up on business and childcare issues. Since "Babysitting 101" wouldn't look very impressive on a transcript, you may want to grant credit using a more academic-sounding course name. Possibilities include:

- Fundamentals of Childcare
- Child Psychology: Concepts and Applications
- Introduction to Entrepreneurship
- Home Economics: Family Management
- Introduction to First Aid

You may even decide to separate the different activities performed in the business and grant fractions of a credit, based upon the number of hours spent. When I was in high school, these mini-courses were called "Special Modules" and were considered electives.

In the same way, the hours your student spends learning HTML to create a web page can be listed as Computer Technology or Web Design. If a teen spends time writing, designing, and illustrating a family or school newsletter, this could be listed as Journalism, Graphic Design, Communication Skills, or simply added to the English Subject Worksheet as part of the student's English credit.

Don't let educational experiences slip by because you can't think where to fit them on the transcript! Even experiences that seem nonacademic, such as vacations, may have elements that could be listed on a Subject Worksheet. Depending on how involved your student is in the planning process, and the type of vacation you take, you may be able to list travel activities in several subjects:

- Geography (navigation/map skills)
- Language Arts (keeping a journal, blogging, writing letters)

- Intercultural Communication (learning about or meeting people from other cultures)

- History (visiting battlefields or historical sites, pre-reading about the destination)

- Physical Education (hiking, skiing, swimming)

- Foreign Language

- Geology (rock collection)

- Art History and Appreciation (visiting museums)

- Health and Safety (treating a sprained ankle and bug bites)

None of these alone will be enough for a complete Carnegie unit, but they can be added to the Subject Worksheets so that the time spent can be counted with other activities in the same subject.

Where to Find More Naming Ideas

If you have a lot of unusual activities, you may need some extra ideas. High-school and college websites, as well as college catalogs, are fertile grounds for class name ideas. College class descriptions are usually more focused and specific than those at the high-school level, so they are the first place I look for inspiration.

> **Tip:** You'll never forget to record an activity if you keep a few 3" x 5" cards with you. You can scribble notes on them when you are away from home, then copy them to the worksheets once you are back at your desk.

Teaching Teens

Charlotte Mason

What must be taught

"First and chiefest is the knowledge of God, to be got at most directly through the Bible; then comes the knowledge of man, to be got through history, literature, art, civics, ethics, biography, the drama, and languages; and lastly, so much knowledge of the universe as shall explain to some extent the phenomena we are familiar with and give a naming acquaintance at any rate with birds and flowers, stars and stones; nor can this knowledge of the universe be carried far in any direction without the ordering of mathematics..."

How to teach it

"... Believe in mind, and let education go straight as a bolt to the mind of the pupil. The use of books is a necessary corollary, because no one is arrogant enough to believe he can teach every subject ... with the original thought and exact knowledge shown by the man who has written a book on ... his life-study ... Treat children in this reasonable way ... the minds of a score of thinkers who meet the children, mind to mind, in their several books, the teacher performing the graceful office of presenting the one enthusiastic mind to the other ... [There must be] a great deal of consecutive reading from very various books, all of some literary value..."

What is the result of this teaching?

"... The introduction of the methods I advocate has a curious effect on a whole family ... The whole household thinks of and figures to itself great things, for nothing is so catching as knowledge ... Children so taught are delightful companions because they have large interests and worthy thoughts; they have much to talk about and such casual talk benefits society. The fine sense, like an atmosphere, of things worth knowing and worth living for, this it is which produces magnanimous citizens, and we feel that Milton was right in claiming magnanimity as the proper outcome of education."

From "A Liberal Education in Secondary Schools" in *A Philosophy of Education* by Charlotte Mason

Grading Ethically: What You Must Know

For many of us, freedom from traditional classroom busywork such as testing and grading is one of the greatest joys of homeschooling. However, this doesn't necessarily make it any easier to create a transcript! It can be intimidating to think of translating all your student's wonderful unit studies, life experiences, volunteer activities, and delight-directed learning into credits and grades by which your student will be judged.

We'll talk about the nuts and bolts of units, grade point averages, and all the other details in the next chapter, but first, it's important to discuss a topic that affects all of us—how to fairly and ethically grade someone you love.

It's critical to understand the traditional meaning and function of grades and their place in the college admissions process, so that you can grade wisely. Although home educators are a diverse group, the actions of each of us affect the reputation of homeschoolers everywhere. Each time a college admissions counselor encounters a homeschooled student whose performance meets or exceeds the expectations created by the grades on his or her transcript, that counselor is likely to perceive homeschoolers as ethical, accurate, and reasonably objective.

How can you provide the kind of grades that achieve this happy result? One way is to begin with the end in mind, as Steven Covey counsels in *The 7 Habits of Highly Successful People*. You need to understand the purpose of the transcript, know what the admissions counselor is looking for, and be aware of the educator's definition of an "A" student.

Traditional Grading Standards

First, the fact is that grading is a practice based upon traditional standards. While colleges are aware of geographic and institutional variables in traditional schools, there are many things that are somewhat standardized. When an admissions officer looks at a group of transcripts, he can assume that potential students who present "A" averages on their transcripts will possess similar learning capacity. Obviously, an "A" earned by a student from a disadvantaged inner-city school will not mean exactly the same as an "A" from a selective, challenging private school, but the grades do indicate the student's basic potential as well as his or her class standing. This gives the admissions officer a basis for comparison.

Home education presents a different set of variables altogether. Each homeschool is unique—we may use traditional textbooks, unit studies, classical education, Charlotte Mason, unschooling, or other options—but the bottom line is that each home and family functions independently, and definitions can be subjective. Therefore, to a college administrator, the homeschool transcript can present a puzzle. What are the standards used to determine grades? How are results measured? How objective can a parent be when grading his or her own child? I would like to present a few points for you to consider as you begin preparing the transcript.

What is the Purpose of the Transcript?

The primary purpose of the transcript is to showcase your student and his or her achievements. This is usually done for the purpose of getting into college, so the audience for the transcript is most often a college admissions counselor. The counselor's goal is to select students who will be a good fit for the college. He needs, at minimum, to know if the student:

- Can perform at an academic level comparable to other students
- Has a talent in the arts, sports, or a particular academic discipline
- Is a well-rounded individual
- Will bring valuable personal qualities to the university
- Seems likely, based upon previous school records, to graduate

It is your job, as the responsible parent who certifies the transcript, to convey this information as carefully and accurately as possible.

What is a Straight-A Student?

Many homeschoolers are what a college would consider genuine "A" students due to wide reading and/or excellent study habits. A genuine "A" student is characterized by a rich vocabulary, intellectual curiosity, the ability to write and speak articulately, a comparatively quick grasp of new material, and the ability to connect new information with old and reach logical conclusions. If this describes your student, his standardized test results, admission essay, and letters of recommendation will probably support a 4.0 grade point average.

Mastery Learning

Some home educators believe in mastery learning. This is basically having the student retake tests and work at a subject until they get all the answers correct, so that they receive an "A." You may choose to do this, but from the perspective of an admissions officer, this type of grading is not accurate. If a student needs multiple retries to pass a test, and extra instruction to grasp a subject, he is, quite frankly, not what an admissions officer (or anyone else) would consider an "A" student. If a student is graded this way, his or her abilities are being misrepresented, and the disparity between his "A" grades and low test scores may cause admissions counselors to question the objectivity of all homeschool-issued diplomas.

If you practice mastery learning and want to award a straight "A" transcript to indicate mastery of each subject, go ahead and do so. Just keep it for your own records, and create a separate transcript for college admissions. You may do this using the Check-Off Transcript. This will allow the admissions counselor to see the subjects you have covered, and let him know that he needs to rely upon the admissions essay and standardized test scores for comparative information. If you don't want to create two transcripts, at least be sure to provide, in the Basic Information section of the transcript, a grading scale or philosophy statement that accurately portrays the criteria you used to determine grades.

Objectivity = Credibility

Admissions office personnel have had enough experience with "helicopter parents" (the ones that won't stop hovering) that they understand the depth of a parent's love. They start off by assuming that very few parents are able to grade objectively, because they want their students to be successful, and they are somewhat blinded by affection for their child. Counselors also realize that most homeschool parents have no other students with whom to compare levels of achievement.

And really, is it possible to be objective about someone you love? I know that it's hard. When you're drafting a document that will present your child to the world in the sterile terms of a grade point average, it can be difficult to stay focused on the fact that the transcript is just a snapshot of a student's academic performance during the high-school years rather than a commentary on his or her entire life (and on our own teaching ability).

As you work with the transcript, you must do your best to be objective without being unnecessarily harsh. It's a balancing act! High-school performance does not necessarily predict future success in life. Even if the student has been less than motivated during the high-school years and didn't work to his potential, the transcript should reflect actual performance. Even if his grade point average isn't what you would like it to be, other factors such as the admissions essay, letters of recommendation, and standardized test scores can help round out the picture of who he really is. On the other hand, performance standards in the public schools are pretty dismal, so be sure you don't establish unrealistic standards for perfection.

Tip: If there is a subject that you are extremely confident in, be sure that you are using realistic standards with your students. I was an English major in college, and it wasn't until I started teaching online English classes, and working with other students, that I discovered I was expecting nearly college-level work from my own boys. I had almost totally skipped over high-school English and was teaching college material to eighth and tenth graders! It seemed perfectly simple to me, and if they hadn't done well, I could have graded too hard and they would have ended up with a lower grade than they deserved.

Standardized Tests: The Key to Objectivity

The good news is that there are objective ways to measure what your student has learned. I call them "Credibility Clinchers" because that's what they're for. Standardized tests are excellent tools for establishing credibility.

For college-bound students, the test path begins with the PSAT, SAT, or ACT and continues with subject-area AP or CLEP exams. Students who aren't headed to college may opt to take the same exams or the GED.

I recommend the college-bound path for all students, not only because it can demonstrate a broader range and greater depth of knowledge but also because if your student later changes his or her mind and wants to go to college, the test scores will be ready to go. In addition, the GED is not well-regarded, as it is most often seen as a last-chance option for students who have dropped out of school.

Because many colleges grant advanced placement, or even credit, for acceptable AP and CLEP scores, taking those exams will give your student a head start on college if he eventually decides to attend. (You can read more about this in my other book, *Get a Jump Start on College! A Practical Guide for Teens*, available from my website at www.getajumpstartoncollege.com.)

When you submit test scores with your student's transcript, you provide information that is easily comparable and obviously objective. It works just as well for unschoolers and relaxed record-keepers as it does for meticulous recorders. Standardized test scores provide a simple, straightforward measurement of knowledge that can validate the entire transcript in the eyes of college admissions officials. Needless to say, I highly recommend them. If your student tends to test badly, you may want to use a community college class or two as credibility clinchers, rather than testing.

Grading and granting credit are often the last things we do as a homeschool parent. Just as you've done throughout your student's school days, do the best you can. If your student has done exceptionally well, don't be afraid to show it on the transcript. If he or she has experienced difficulty, grade honestly, but with love and mercy. If you doubt your ability to grade objectively, ask for help. A more experienced home educator, a support group leader, or even a professional homeschool consultant may be able to help. You'll find that it's not nearly as hard as it seems!

A genuine 'A' student is characterized by a rich vocabulary, intellectual curiosity, the ability to write and speak articulately, a comparatively quick grasp of new material, and the ability to connect new information with old and reach logical conclusions.

How to Grade and Grant Credit

As you prepare to create your student's transcript, you will need to assign grades for each class, unless you are an unschooler and plan to include a nongrading philosophy on your transcript. I have to confess that I never assigned grades to my students' daily work—I just didn't feel that it was useful or necessary. However, I did informal evaluations[1] throughout the semester that allowed me to confidently assign a semester grade when I filled out their transcript.

It's obvious how to grade simple assignments such as vocabulary worksheets, math problems, or multiple-choice exams, but written assignments can be more difficult to evaluate. I'll explain briefly how I evaluate writing, but I hope you'll remember that there is no "one right way." Methods and reasoning differ from homeschool to home-

---

[1]When I say "informal evaluation" that's exactly what I mean. I would look over an assignment and decide whether it looked as if the student "got it," if he did a great job, or if he needed more work. Very basic!

school, and even from private schools to public schools, and from public schools to charter schools. There are many ways to evaluate, and these suggestions are only what I have found practical and reasonable.

How to Evaluate Written Work

Written work, such as essays, reports, and summaries, is evaluated on several levels, and it's a bit harder to do than just matching answers to an answer sheet! There is usually no "one perfect way to say it," particularly in literary analysis, but there are some basic areas that should be evaluated for each assignment. These are summarized in the 6+1 Trait° Evaluation from Northwest Regional Educational Laboratory (www.nwrel.org). This system is a good way to be sure that you're objectively evaluating every area that needs to be checked in each assignment.

The six traits, along with very brief comments on the scope of each trait, are:

- **Ideas and Content:** Look for a strong thesis and focused, accurate content with interesting, appropriate details.

- **Organization:** Is the piece logically organized with an obvious sequence of supporting information?

- **Voice:** Does the writing sound as if it's composed by a real person who is engaged with the topic?

- **Word Choice:** Look for vivid, precise language, accurately used, that shows, rather than tells.

- **Sentence Fluency:** Read aloud a paragraph. Does it flow? Sentences should vary in length and style, as appropriate for the content.

- **Conventions:** This trait is sometimes known as "mechanics," and it includes grammar, spelling, and punctuation. This trait should be fairly well mastered by high school, and students should be in the habit of automatically grammar- and spell-checking all papers in addition to proofreading before they turn them in. You should see very few errors in Conventions!

An additional trait that is sometimes included with the six traits (the "plus one" in 6+1 Trait°) is Presentation—how the work looks. Once students are in high school,

I require that all papers be typed in college format (one-inch margins, double spaced, Times New Roman font). It's the best way to prepare them for college!

If you do a Google search for "writing rubric" you will come up with several sample rubrics (a rubric is a checklist of objective standards) that will help you grade writing assignments. You may also find more detailed instructions for evaluating in my short booklet *Evaluate Writing the Easy Way* (www.EvaluateWriting.com) Using a rubric allows you to quickly and realistically evaluate a writing assignment and provide specific, helpful feedback so that the student will understand what he did well and what skill areas need to be improved.

How to Grant Credit

When your student has completed the assignments listed on the Class Profile, it is time to grant credit for the class. Although we speak of granting "credit," the traditional measurement of high-school achievement is the Carnegie unit (colleges award "credits"). When we award a Carnegie *unit,* the students' hard work is being acknowledged; they are receiving "credit" for their efforts. I hope that's clear!

A class that lasts for one 16- to 18-week semester is worth a half unit, which would appear on a transcript as 0.5. A two-semester, 32- to 36-week class will earn one unit. Thus, a two-semester class worth one unit would equal 120 to 180 hours of study, depending upon your state requirements, if any.

1 Carnegie unit = 1 full-year course
or
1 unit = 120–180 classroom hours of study (a classroom hour is 50–60 minutes)
or
50–60 minutes/day x 5 days/week x 36 weeks

Some states specify that one unit or credit must equal at least 120 hours of "guided instruction,"[2] so if your state homeschool law requires the education you provide to be "equivalent" to this standard, be sure that the grading scale you specify on your transcript reflects this minimum specification.

---

[2]Guided instruction includes any work done in response to instruction, including listening, reading, writing, and lab assignments.

But What If We Don't Study by the Clock?

Practically speaking, it is unlikely that you or your teen records the minutes spent on each subject. Fortunately, it's unnecessary! There is a much easier way to keep track of units earned. Most textbooks are designed to be completed in one school year; therefore, when the textbook is finished (most traditional schools consider textbooks "completed" when about 80% of lessons have been done), you may grant credit. It couldn't be simpler!

1 unit/credit = one completed textbook

How to Grant Credit for Unit Studies

Most formal unit-study publishers, such as KONOS, provide a breakdown of exactly how credit may be awarded for completion of the study. For unit studies that have no written guidelines, you may grant credit based upon the number of weeks the student was involved with the study. For example, if a study lasts for twelve weeks, that is one-third of the school year, so you would grant ⅓ unit for each subject covered. Many unit studies include history, English, art, and literature—you would grant ⅓ credit for each of these subjects.

1 unit/credit = 1 year unit study

> **Tip**: What you are certifying by granting credit is that the student has studied a specific body of knowledge, not that he knows all there is to know about the subject.

How to Define a Grading Scale

If you provide grades, your transcript should define what level of performance each letter grade represents. Even if you didn't do anything more than the informal

Most textbooks are designed to be completed in one school year; therefore, when the textbook is finished (most traditional schools consider textbooks "completed" when about 80% of lessons have been done), you may grant credit.

evaluations I mentioned earlier, you can usually estimate whether your student's work is superior, average, or below average. The verbal and percentage definitions provided below are just suggestions. You may adjust the percentages to match your local schools or use any other words you'd prefer to define your standards for performance.

Grading Scale and Quality Point Suggestions					
Letter Grade	Verbal Definition	Percentage Definition	Quality Points	Honors Points	AP/College Points
A	Superior	92–100%	4	4.5	5
B	Above Average	84–91%	3	3.5	4
C	Satisfactory	76–83%	2	2.5	3
D	Below Average	68–75%	1	1.5	2

Once you have decided on the letter grade your student will receive, you need to assign a numerical value (quality points or grade points) to each letter grade. This is quite simple, as you can see in the chart above. However you describe your letter grades, your student will receive four quality points for an "A," three for a "B," two for a "C," and one for a "D," unless the course is an honors or AP (college-equivalent) course. If you issue only Pass/Fail or Complete/Incomplete grades (something I don't recommend unless you have no other option), you will not provide quality points.

Weighted Grades

AP or honors courses and exams can be given weighted grades, which are simply extra grade points. A grade for an honors class would receive an extra half point, and a grade for an AP or college-level course would receive an extra whole point. This means that an honors student who earns an "A" would receive 4.5 quality points, while a student who passes a college-level class, AP exam, or CLEP exam would receive 5 quality points for an "A." You can see an example of how this works on the filled-out transcript samples later in the book.

Because an honors class covers more material in greater depth than a standard high-school course, and many students opt to take college-level classes to earn Advanced

Placement (AP) credit, the weighted grade point system was developed. The extra quality points are granted in recognition of the intensity of the study.

Some colleges like to see weighted grades, while others do not (you can read some un-varnished opinions about this in the Counselor interviews). Because most traditional schools provide weighted grades, homeschoolers may as well use them too. It's just another way to level the playing field (or tilt it in our favor!). Most colleges recalculate grade point averages anyway, so if the college of your choice doesn't use weighted grades, the counselor can refigure the student's GPA using a standard grading scale.

Granting Credit for AP, Dual Credit, or College-Equivalent Classes

If you are awarding dual credit (actually, you are granting the high-school units, while the college credit is granted by your student's college), remember that you are granting credit for material covered, not time spent. Even though it's called dual credit, your only concern is the high-school part of the credit. The college credits you record on the Subject Worksheets will have been awarded by the college where the student is enrolled, and they will appear on his or her college transcript as transfer credit. The Carnegie units you grant will appear on the high-school transcript.

"... you are granting credit for material covered, not time spent."

If your student takes a one-semester college class that covers an entire textbook on a subject such as college algebra, he earns one whole Carnegie unit for the class (just as he would if he finished a high-school textbook) and receives two semester's worth of weighted grade points because the textbook concepts are designed to be covered in two semesters. Most college classes cover an entire book in a semester, but if the student takes a one-semester class that covers only half a textbook and then a class that completes the textbook, he would earn half a Carnegie unit and weighted grade points for each semester of the class.

The way you list these classes on the transcript differs according to which transcript style you choose. I think the Subject-Order transcript is one of the simplest to use if you have earned a lot of credit by exam or through college classes. You can list each course with its corresponding exam or college class, and award credit appropriately, according to the chart below. You'll notice in the sample that:

- English I is an ordinary class, earning 0.5 of a unit and 4 quality points per semester.
- English II is an honors class, earning 0.5 of a unit and 4.5 quality points per semester.

- English III and IV are college-level classes, with a six-credit CLEP as a final exam. The percentile ranking of the CLEP score is taken into consideration when awarding a grade, and because each of these exams covers material that is normally covered in a two-semester college class, you have a couple of options.

  - One option is to award one Carnegie unit with corresponding quality points for every three college credits earned. You can see this option used in the Western Civilization courses listed. The student earned a total of two units and twenty quality points over a period of four semesters for this study. If you choose this option, it is usually best to list the class as two separate classes, as in "Western Civilization I and Western Civilization II."

  - A second option is to award one Carnegie unit plus appropriate quality points for each college course or six-credit exam. This option is shown in the listing for English III and IV. The student earned one unit and ten quality points over two semesters for each of these classes.

Which option to choose is really a judgement call. While both the English III and IV and the Western Civilization courses and exams cover material equivalent to what would be learned in two semesters of a college class, you may cover one subject in a great deal more depth than the other. If you have spent four semesters covering the material, as in the Western Civilization example, I would award one unit for every three college credits. If you have spent only two semesters mastering the material, as in each of the English classes, I would award one unit for each two-semester class. Use your best judgement, and if the college wants to tweak your numbers, they will do so.

The Vertical Transcript sample in the back provides another example of how weighted grades can be applied to a specific class. You will notice that the study of Western Civilization covers two years, earning two Carnegie units (equal to 120 hours of instruction each) plus five weighted grade points for each semester of this advanced, writing-intensive class. The student received college-level quality points for this course because he passed the CLEP exams, which confirmed that his knowledge was equivalent to what he would have learned in a college class. If he had done the same amount of work but had not passed the CLEP exams, he would have been awarded Honors points (half of a quality point).

Honors Classes

Honors classes are usually weighted by half a grade point, reflecting an advanced level of difficulty in the class assignments. These classes are more in-depth than the average high-school class, but not as difficult as a college class.

Granting Credit for Special Classes			
If your student takes...	It would equal...	The college would award...	You would record on the transcript....
1-semester college class (example: American History 101)	2 semesters of high-school study	3 college credits	1 Carnegie unit plus weighted grade points
2-semester AP class with AP exam	2 semesters of high-school study	Advanced Placement (some colleges may also award credit)	1 Carnegie unit plus weighted grade points
College-level exam covering 1 semester of study (example: college algebra)	2 semesters of high-school study	3 college credits	1 Carnegie unit plus weighted grade points
College-level exam covering 2 semesters of college study (any of the 6-credit exams.)	4 semesters of high-school study	6 college credits	2 Carnegie units plus weighted grade points
Remember: you grant only high-school credits (Carnegie units) on your transcript. College credit will appear on the student's college transcript.			
Credit-by-Exam will appear on the college transcript whenever your student enrolls in a college and requests that the exam transcript be sent to the college.			

How to Figure a Grade Point Average

There are three basic steps to follow in calculating a grade point average (GPA) for a semester:

How to Grade and Grant Credit

1. Assign grade points (a numerical value) to each grade you have given for each class. The traditional numbers are: A = 4, B = 3, C = 2, D = 1, F = 0. For AP or honors-level classes, including college-level courses, assign weighted grade points—that is, add one extra grade point for each grade. This would make the value of "A" equal to 5, "B" equal to 4, and so forth.

2. Add together all the grade points for each class (except physical education, which is not usually included in the calculation of the GPA).

3. Divide the total grade points by the total number of classes taken.

The result will be the grade point average for the semester. If this seems confusing, just look at the sample below. It sounds more complex than it really is.

Example

If a student has two A's (worth 4 grade points each), two B's (worth 3 grade points each), and two C's (worth 2 grade points each) in a semester, and wants to calculate a grade point average (GPA), this is how it's done:

Add grade points:	Add the sums:	Divide the number of grade points (18) by the number of classes taken (6).
2 A's = 4 + 4 = 8		
2 B's = 3 + 3 = 6	8 + 6 + 4 = 18	18 / 6 = 3.0 GPA
2 C's = 2 + 2 = 4		

To calculate a cumulative GPA, add together all the grade points earned in each semester, and divide the total by the number of Carnegie units earned.

Free GPA Calculator

If you'd like a super-easy alternative to calculating your grade point average on a calculator (and I realize that's not very hard!), just visit www.freegpacalc.com. I have posted two calculators there for you to use. The first one calculates the semester grade point average, while the second one calculates the cumulative average. To use the semester calculator, just select the letter grade you want for each class from the drop-down menu. You may choose a standard or weighted grade for each individual class. When you've selected all the grades for the semester, just click the 'calculate' button, and record the average. When you are ready to calculate a cumulative grade point average, go down to the second calculator and enter each semester average, along with the number of units earned, in the boxes provided. Click 'calculate' once more, and you have a total cumulative average and total number of units earned. Now, wasn't that easy?

Tip: Grade points for physical education are not usually calculated into the GPA.

Not everything that can be counted counts, and not everything that counts can be counted.

Albert Einstein

Transcripts for Unschoolers and the Chronically Relaxed

I f you are an unschooler or a relaxed homeschooler and don't grade your students, you have several options. You may decide to state your philosophy on the transcript and not provide grades at all; you may use the Check-Off Transcript style with a Pass/Fail evaluation system; or you may decide to create a portfolio.

Non-Grading Philosophy

You may use the Basic Information space on the transcript to briefly explain your philosophy. All you need is a brief paragraph. For example: "We at Stagg Creek Family School have chosen a cooperative, rather than competitive, learning paradigm. Our students have learned to do their best at whatever subject they begin, and we award credit when it is apparent that the student has attained mastery of the subject.

Therefore, we have found it unnecessary to use letter grades." Place this paragraph, or something similar, in the space provided for the Grading Scale.

Check-Off Transcript with Pass/Fail Evaluations

If you are structured enough to create a course list using the worksheets, the check-off type of transcript shown in Sample 4 in the Transcript chapter may suit your learning philosophy. This sample was adapted from a transcript developed by Mary Baldwin College for homeschoolers. It permits students to simply check off the subjects they have covered, though there is room to indicate Pass or Fail or to include grades if you decide to do so.

Portfolios

If your course of study was so relaxed that you can't translate it into a traditional list of courses, you may want to consider a portfolio instead of a transcript. In *Homeschooling for Excellence*, David and Micki Colfax briefly describe the papers they submitted with their homeschooled son's college application. These included a "letter … describing his course work and evaluating his strengths and weaknesses as objectively as possible," a long autobiographical essay by the student, and letters of recommendation from several people who had worked with him. This portfolio, along with outstanding standardized test scores, was apparently quite adequate, for he was accepted to both Yale and Harvard.

That said, most college admissions departments do not have time to look at portfolios. I worked part-time in an admissions department for a couple of years, and I can attest to the astonishing workload teetering on the desks of the admissions counselors. Each counselor receives hundreds of applications to sift through, and they are quickly sorted into "yes," "no," "maybe," and "I don't even want to look at this" piles. Prospective students who want to end up in the "yes" or "maybe" pile can make the counselor's job a lot easier by condensing all their wonderful experiences into a tidy transcript that can be easily compared to others.

If you really want to go with a portfolio, however, the Colfax's ingredients (above) sound just about right. You may wish to include a sample reading log and/or a list of extracurricular activities. I would suggest compiling the documents into a half-inch three-ring binder with page protectors. Once you have it all together, be sure to provide a table of contents at the front of the binder so the admissions counselor can quickly turn to the pages most important to him or her.

Retrospective Grading

If you have followed a more traditional course of study but haven't used grades through the high-school years, it's still possible to assign grades if you find your student needs a grade point average. The most objective way to do this is by having the student take AP or CLEP exams in each of the basic subject areas.

If your student is not college-bound, you can also base grades upon the student's overall performance in a subject, rather than the traditional accumulation of individual test and assignment grades. If you want to provide grades based upon overall performance, rather than traditional Carnegie units, be sure to indicate this in the Basic Information section of the transcript. When you think about the letter grade that best fits, consider the following factors:

- Difficulty of the course material
- Progress demonstrated by the student
- Quality of work completed
- Quality of effort expended
- Citizenship factors such as attitude, neatness, and punctuality

The accuracy of retrospective grading depends largely upon the quality of your memory or your records. If you have difficulty remembering details of a specific class, your teen may be able to help. If you're doing this at the end of high school, you'll probably know whether your student is average in math, superior in English, or above average in science, and this knowledge can translate into letter grades:

A = Superior/Outstanding

B = Above Average/Good

C = Average/Satisfactory

D = Below Average/Unsatisfactory

Retrospectively assigned grades can be evaluated for objectivity by considering whether the student's standardized test scores seem to confirm the grade level you have assigned to his work. It is better to issue a transcript as simply a list of subjects, as in Sample 4 on page 81, than to issue grades that aren't supported by other evidence.

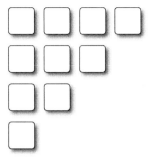

Records and Transcripts for Special-Needs Students

Students with special needs often thrive in a homeschool environment. The individualized attention they receive can help them progress despite learning difficulties. Some special-needs students are able to follow a traditional course of study with a few minor modifications in coursework or testing, while others with more severe disabilities must follow a course of study that has been adapted to their needs.

Because I have no personal experience with special-needs students, I interviewed Judith Munday (M.A., M.Ed., a Virginia-Licensed Educational Consultant, Endorsed for K–12 Learning Disabilities) via e-mail. Here are my questions, and Judi's responses:

JPC: If a student has been diagnosed as a special-needs student, should parents include this information on the transcript?

JM: This depends on whether parents want the student to have his or her special needs met by accommodations in higher education. Such accommodations to meet special needs are legally allowable and required under federal law if the college/school gets ANY federal money (including Pell grants).

It is becoming increasingly common for universities and colleges to have robust student services for students who needed extra support to achieve success in high school. Even standardized tests such as the SAT can be taken with specific accommodations IF the student has met specified requirements. One requirement is that the specific learning disability/special need must be documented by someone with appropriate credentials. Counselors want to ensure the student did not suddenly develop a special need to give him or her a better chance for success in college admissions! :-o Yes, I guess it does happen.

It would be impossible to cite all the variables here, so my advice to parents of college-bound and community-college-bound students is to check each school's website for information about allowable accommodations for testing and services available during the educational years. Parents or students may have to dig a bit within a given website to find information, or they can simply call the college or SAT offices. Contact information can be found at the Princeton Review website, among other places.

JPC: Is it a good idea to identify the specific disability or special need on the transcript?

JM: Certainly it will have to be if the student needs documentation for college admission or special considerations during attendance. The allowable accommodations are based upon the specific needs. The more specific the documentation, the more access to appropriate help at college will be available. These accommodations can range from having scribes take down dictated test answers for a student with dysgraphia or it may just mean extra time for testing! In order to qualify for accommodations, the disabilities must be documented by fully qualified professionals. Some colleges and test situations have more stringent requirements than others. In every case, however, the parents' word alone will not suffice to identify the student's special need.

Records and Transcripts for Special-Needs Students

JPC: Is a student with special needs required to follow any sort of formal plan for his or her education?

JM: The student who has special needs in the homeschool is not required to have a special educational plan (SEP). However, I still recommend special-needs homeschool students have an SEP. It gives a parent the opportunity to form realistic annual goals, and it outlines a means of accountability and provides a way to assess progress at regular intervals during the year. It can also be the end-of-year standard against which to measure the child's achievement. (This can be really helpful for severely disabled students or those whose level is more vocational or life-skills based.)

JPC: Who creates the SEP?

JM: Parents can create their own SEP, but for students with severe, diagnosed disabilities, a qualified education consultant can provide an appropriate SEP.

JPC: Is an SEP the same as an IEP?

JM: IEP (Individualized Education Plan) is a term reserved for those documents created by public schools for public-school students. It lists services that will be paid for by public education funds earmarked to provide special services. It is not appropriate for homeschoolers to use this term for their own student education plans.

JPC: Should the transcript show that the student has been following an SEP?

JM: Since many special-needs students are not on grade level as they progress into high school, they are not always going to be taking high school difficulty-level coursework. Sometimes, they will not be taking all their courses at the same grade level, for example, taking seventh grade math at the same time as they are taking twelfth grade English. I believe for college-bound homeschooled students, the SEP would represent to a college admissions officer that the parent had made an effort to set responsibly high standards and that they had incorporated educational best practices in teaching the child.

Tip from JPC: I would suggest placing this information in the Basic Information section of the transcript, under the heading Grading Scale. Rather than putting in the usual grading scale information, simply put "See attached Student Education Plan." The Check-Off-style transcript would work particularly well for a special-needs student.

JPC: Are special-needs students required to take the same standardized tests as other students?

JM: HSLDA reminds us that in some states we can use Assessments or Evaluations for year-end assessments instead of standardized tests. These can be a bit fuzzy for documentation and transcripts without some terminal standard, which the SEP can provide. National aptitude exams such as the SAT or ACT can be taken with special accommodations such as extra time or reading/writing help.

JPC: Should the parent inform the public-school system of a special-needs diagnosis or the existence of an SEP?

JM: HSLDA folks I've spoken with recommend that parents not provide the public school with any SEP copies or information nor should parents identify the child as having special needs. There are some counties I've heard of where declarations of special needs can almost trigger Social Service visits—others welcome the information and are supportive. It is certainly safer to use licensed, private consultants for special-needs services.

You may contact Judi through her website, www.hishelpinschool.com

Judith B. Munday, M.A., M.Ed., Educational Consultant
Virginia Licensed, Endorsed K–12 Learning Disabilities

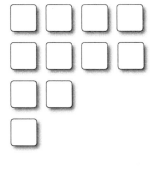

What Goes on the Transcript and Diploma?

Before you begin your transcript, let's talk about each of its parts. Once you understand all that goes on it (and see that the explanation is much longer than what you need to come up with), you'll realize that it's not nearly as challenging as it might seem. This is something you can do!

There are three major sections on every transcript: the Identity section, Basic Information section, and Course Record section. Here's an overview of what each part contains, followed by a detailed breakdown of what goes where:

1. **Identity:** This section of the transcript identifies the document, the student, the school, and the date of graduation.

2. **Basic Information:** In this part of the transcript, you'll define your grading scale or nongrading philosophy, the number of hours that equals a unit, and the abbreviations used for credit by exam or dual-credit classes. The signature of the certifying parent should also appear here.

3. **Course Record:** This is the body of the transcript—your final record of all the courses your student has completed during the high-school years.

Part One: Identity

The transcript begins by identifying what it is. If you look at a dozen different transcripts, you'll find a variety of titles:

High School Transcript

Official Homeschool Transcript

Private School Transcript

Transcript

Stagg Creek High School Transcript

I point this out so that you'll be comfortable choosing the title you prefer. There is no "right" title, no one-size-fits-all format, just as there is no one-size-fits-all homeschool. Choose what you prefer, and use it with confidence.

Student Information

This section provides information about the student's identity while he was in high school. If, for example, you are a bit late in getting the transcript created, and your daughter has married, you will still put her maiden name on the transcript because that is the name she used while in high school.

Student's Name

Use the student's full legal name. It is your decision whether to list it in filing order (last name first) or first name first. You will see it both ways on the samples.

Date of Birth

Use numerals for this, usually MM/DD/YYYY.

What Goes on the Transcript and Diploma?

Social Security Number

This is optional, and I do not use it on my sons' transcripts. The school to which your student applies will need the SSN for their records, but it will be requested with other paperwork. Since high-school transcripts are sometimes submitted with scholarship applications, I prefer to keep the SSN off the transcript in order to limit the possibility of misuse.

Gender

Optional, but recommended if the student's name is not gender-specific (Leslie, Tyler, Beverly).

Parents

Another optional line. If you choose to list your names, list them in legal format (Henry R. and Katherine T. Ford) rather than social format (Mr. and Mrs. Hank Ford).

Admission Date

Optional. Also referred to as "Date of Entry," this is just the date when your student began high-school work. If the number of years your student spent in school is significantly different from the expected four-year timeframe for completing high-school work, I suggest not including this date. If you do include it, use the MM/YYYY format.

Graduation Date

The date when the student completed the required number of credits for high-school graduation. Use the same format as the Admission Date.

Grade Point Average

This can appear in Part One or Part Three or not at all if you choose to use the course-list format in Sample 4.

School Information

If you haven't decided on a name for your school before now, you can make a quick decision, or you can just choose to identify your school as "Homeschool." Again, there is no legal or traditional requirement to influence your decision.

School Name

This is what you call your own homeschool. Do not use the name of your curriculum provider (e.g., Bob Jones High School), any name that could be confused with your local public high school, or any other name that would imply connection with an official organization (e.g., Virginia SOL Academy). You may use:

- Your last name (Campbell High School)
- Your street name (Connor Avenue Preparatory School)
- A local geographic feature (Stagg Creek High School)
- A descriptive name (Great Books Private School)
- A religious name (Living Word Christian Academy)

You may select anything that you feel effectively describes your school and does not infringe upon the identity of another institution.

School Address

This is the only address information that appears on the transcript, because transcripts are requested from schools, not from students. This is because students are assumed to have moved on in life, while schools usually remain in the same place.

Telephone Number

Optional, but useful if the admissions department needs more information.

E-mail or Web Address

Optional, but recommended. I suggest including both parent and student e-mails, plus a web address if you have an educational website. I don't advise including blog addresses, as most are not designed to impress college officials!

Previous School

If the student began high school enrolled in a public or private school, list the name and address here. The transcript you issue will cover only the years you actually taught your student, so the college you choose will have to request a transcript from any other school attended.

This is the end of the Identity section (you'll notice that the explanation was a lot longer than the actual section!). However you design your document, this section will usually be at the top. Be sure each element is easy to find and identify, as in the sample transcripts.

Part Two: Basic Information

In order to fill out this section, you will refer to the chapter on Grading, along with your state's homeschool law, in order to determine:

- Grading scale or nongrading philosophy
- The number of hours that equals a unit
- Key to the abbreviations used for credit by exam or dual-credit classes

This section also includes a line for the signature of the certifying parent or parents.

Part Three: Course Record

Although this section has the shortest description, it's the main part of the transcript! The Course Record is the listing of classes that forms the body of the transcript. In this section, you will condense the information from Class Profiles and Subject Worksheets into a concise list of your student's high-school course of study. You can look at the sample transcripts for help and ideas as you fill out your own.

Practical Tips for Creating the Transcript

Now you know the three main parts of the transcript and you have enough information to get started. You may want to photocopy a blank sample form and type in your information, but I strongly recommend following the simple instructions for creating the form on your computer. It is much easier to create the basic form, and fill it in as you go, than to try to fit your information into a photocopied form.

Design Basics

Fonts: Use basic, no-frills fonts such as Times New Roman or Arial Narrow. Save the fancy script fonts for the diploma! Primary information, such as identity and course descriptions should be in at least 10 point type; secondary information, such as the grading scale, can be 8 point or even slightly smaller if necessary. Just be sure it's legible. Some fonts are narrower than others, so experiment to see which allows you to attractively squeeze in the most information.

Italics: Do not use an underlined font for anything—it looks dated and unprofessional. Italicize items, such as book titles, that were underlined in the pre-desktop-publishing era.

Bold type: The sparing use of bold type can effectively highlight headings and other significant information.

Paper: Use good-quality, cream or light gray paper when you print out official copies of the transcript. Office supply stores such as OfficeMax or Staples sell packages of resume-quality paper, or you can take it to a local copy store to have it copied onto appropriate paper. Just remember that a transcript is like a resume—you don't want anything cute or too busy. Nonwhite paper is normally used because it doesn't always copy well, so theoretically it can't be altered or forged easily.

The second page: While the transcript is ideally one page, you may have a lot of information to include. If you are about to run onto a second page, here are some suggestions:

Copy and paste the first page onto a blank second page, so that the Identity and Basic Information sections will appear on both pages.

If you are using a transcript format that is categorized by semester, put two years on each page, and stretch the tables to fit the page (click on the edge of the table, hold down the left mouse button, and drag the edge to resize).

Try changing font sizes and font styles to pull the document back to one page. Arial Narrow is a nice clear font that works well in tight spaces.

Remember: think simple, uncluttered, and professional, rather than fancy or decorative. Just as in a resume, the focus should be on the information rather than an elaborate format. I have included complete instructions to help you create your transcript in your choice of formats.

Any of the transcripts, as well as the diploma, can be created in Microsoft Word or any other word-processing program that has the ability to create tables. If you don't have a full-featured word-processing program, I recommend Open Office, an excellent multiplatform program, similar to Microsoft Office, that you may download free from www.openoffice.org.

How to Issue an Official Transcript

When your student needs an "official" copy of his transcript for a college or scholarship application, print a copy on good-quality nonwhite paper (see the previous page for more details) and sign the certification line in blue or black ink. Fold the transcript in thirds and seal in a business-size envelope. You may also sign across the flap of the envelope to demonstrate that the certified transcript has not been opened or tampered with, though this is not usually necessary.

Remember, an official transcript is:

- Printed on "official" nonwhite paper
- Signed (certified) by one or both parents
- Sealed in an envelope sent from the school, not from the student

The Diploma

I did quite a bit of research in the process of revising this book, and I was surprised to find that more people worry about the high-school diploma than about the transcript. I'm not sure why this is—the diploma is simply a ceremonial document, much like a certificate, that acknowledges the fact that the student has completed high school. It has no practical use at all!

If you think about your own high-school diploma, you will know what I mean. Where is it? Has anyone ever asked to see it? My own high-school diploma is neatly packed away in a box in my attic along with other certificates and awards. It is very nice to receive a certificate honoring an achievement, but the certificate has no value in itself. It is the achievement that is important, and in the case of school, the achievement is documented in detail on the transcript.

I think that some of the concern I heard expressed about the high-school diploma may have been the result of using the word "diploma" as a synonym for completing high school. For example, if you are asked whether you have a high-school diploma, the inquirer is not concerned about whether you know where a piece of paper is but whether you have completed high school. If you have completed high school, you can confidently answer "yes!" to that question, even if you no longer have the piece of paper that certifies your achievement.

I have provided a sample diploma form at the end of this chapter. As you will see, the traditional wording is very simple. To re-create the form on your own computer, just follow these simple steps:

1. Open a new document in your word-processing program.

2. Set the document margins to 0.5". You can usually do this in the Document Set-up menu, which is accessed from the File menu.

3. In the Document Set-up menu, select "Landscape" layout, which is usually an icon showing the paper with the long measurement running horizontally. (Most documents are set up in "Portrait Mode," in which the short measurement is horizontal.)

4. Type in the text below (or copy and paste, if you are working from the e-book), substituting appropriate information for filler text. Use a traditional font such as Times New Roman or Garamond.

5. Select each line of text and change the font to the size indicated in the parentheses at the end of each line.

6. Below the last line of text, add the signature lines, about 2" long. Place one at the left margin, and tab forward to place the next one at the right margin.

7. If you want a special font for the first line, a traditional calligraphic style, such as Old English or Lucida Blackletter, looks very traditional.

8. Select all the text (from the Edit menu) and center it. You will usually do this by clicking on an icon that shows a group of lines centered in a box or by choosing "Center" in an Alignment menu.

9. Look at it, and add spaces between the lines to make the spacing pleasing to the eye.

10. Print it and sign in blue or black ink.

Text for Diploma

High School Diploma

What Goes on the Transcript and Diploma?

(large font, sometimes Old English or Blackletter: 24–36 point)

This certifies that
(small font: 14–18 point)

Student's Name
(largest font on the page: 36–48 point)

has completed a College Preparatory Course of Study at
(small font: 14–18 point)

School Name
(medium font: 24–28 point)

and is therefore awarded this Diploma
(small font: 14–18 point)

and is entitled to all the Rights and Privileges appertaining thereunto.
(small font: 14–18 point)

Certified, this [number] day of [month, year] by
(small font: 14–18 point)

Parent Signatures
(handwritten: one at the right margin, one at the left)

High School Diploma

This certifies that

A. Wonderful Student

has completed a College Preparatory Course of Study at

Name of Homeschool

and is therefore awarded this Diploma

and is therefore entitled to all the Rights and Privileges appertaining thereto.

Certified this

9th day of June 2010, by

Parent Signature

Parent Signature

Sample Transcripts and Diploma

Finally, you're ready to begin creating the transcript! Here are the samples that will serve as models for you. You will see that there are four layouts to choose from. There is no "one right way" to create a transcript, so feel free to mix and match elements if you are comfortable doing so. If you don't have a lot of computer experience, just choose the design you like best and closely follow the instructions for creating it. You'll be amazed at how easy it really is!

I have included a filled-out sample here and a blank copy of each transcript in the back of the book, plus basic instructions for re-creating the designs on your computer. In writing these instructions, I am assuming that you know how to use the basic functions of a word-processing program. If not, you might want to ask someone else—perhaps your student—for help.

Sample 1: Horizontal Transcript

This is my favorite format (see it on page 75), and it's designed so that once it's set up, your information can be entered by tabbing from field to field (cell to cell within the table). You won't have to worry at all about alignment and spacing, because the table makes it happen!

Here is how you can create this design in a word-processing program. If you are an experienced computer user, you can skip most of the detail. If you're less confident, I think you'll find that these instructions are an easy introduction to your word-processing program. Just work step-by-step, and before you know it, you'll have a beautiful transcript.

Create and Set Up Document

1. From the File menu, select "New" to create a blank document for the transcript.
2. Go back to the File menu and choose "Page Setup." Set all margins to 0.5". Ignore your program if it tells you these are outside the printable area, because they usually are not.
3. Save your document, giving it a descriptive file name such as the student's initials followed by "Transcript."
4. Go to the Table menu and activate "Show Gridlines. (If the menu says "Hide Gridlines." simply click on it so that it says "Show Gridlines" instead.) This will enable you to see all the table lines as you work, but the grid will not print. When you finish creating the transcript, you can hide the gridlines and see what it will look like when it's printed.

Create Tables

1. Choose "Insert Table" from the Table menu and create a table with 11 columns and 45 rows. Select "Autofit to Contents" and click "OK."
2. Go to the first cell of the second row. Click in it and highlight it and the cell to its right, as well as the 2 cells underneath them, so that you have formed a small square made up of the 4 cells. Go to the Table menu, select "Merge Cells," and type "High School Transcript" in the newly merged cells.
3. Highlight and merge the remaining column in the second and third rows of the table, then type the student's name. Hit return and type the student's date of birth.

Sample Transcripts and Diploma

Connor Hanes
Date of Birth: 10/24/2001

HIGH SCHOOL TRANSCRIPT

School:
Stagg Creek High School
1300 Stagg Creek Drive
Ashland, Virginia 23005
888-123-4567
www.EverydayEducation.com
Admission: 08/2014
Graduation: 12/2017

Fall Semesters

Course Description	Grade	Units Earned	Quality Points
Fall 2014			
English I: Literature & Composition	A	.5	4
Algebra 1/2	B	.5	3
American History	A	.5	4
Earth Science	A	.5	4
Physical Education: Volleyball	B	.5	0
Choir: Mixed Chorus	A	.5	4
Semester Total		3	19
Fall 2015			
English II: American Literature	A	.5	4
Algebra I	B	.5	3
Western Civilization I	B	.5	4*
Biology I	A	.5	4
Physical Education: Swimming	B	.5	0
CSC 155 Computer Concepts and Applications (JSRCC)	B	1	8*
Semester Total		3.5	23
Fall 2016			
English III: British Literature	A	.5	4
Algebra II	B	.5	3
Western Civilization II	A	.5	5*
Chemistry I	A	.5	4
Physical Education: Football	B	.5	0
Choir: Quartet Arrangements	A	.5	4
Semester Total		3	20
Fall 2017			
English IV: World Literature	A	.5	4
Analysis and Interpretation of Literature (CLEP)	A	1	10*
MTH 166 Pre-Calculus With Trigonometry (JSRCC)	C	1	6*
Government and Politics (CLEP)	A	.5	5*
French I (JSRCC)	B	1	8*
Applied Music: Piano	B	.5	3
Semester Total		4.5	36

Spring Semesters

Course Description	Grade	Units Earned	Quality Points
Spring 2015			
English I: Literature & Composition	A	.5	4
Algebra 1/2	B	.5	3
American History	A	.5	4
Earth Science	A	.5	4
Physical Education: Softball	A	.5	0
Art History and Appreciation	A	.5	4
Semester Total		3	19
Cumulative Total		6	38
Spring 2016			
English II: American Literature	A	.5	4
Algebra I	B	.5	3
Western Civilization I (CLEP)	A	.5	5*
Biology I	B	.5	4
Physical Education: Soccer	B	.5	0
Choir: Mixed and Men's Chorus	A	.5	4
Semester Total		3	20
Cumulative Total		12.5	81
Spring 2017			
English III: British Literature	A	.5	4
Algebra II	B	.5	3
Western Civilization II (CLEP)	A	.5	5*
Chemistry I	A	.5	4
Physical Education: Horseback Riding	B	.5	0
Applied Music: Individual Vocal Instruction	A	.5	4
Semester Total		3	20
Cumulative Total		18.5	121
Spring 2018			
English IV: World Literature (JSRCC)	A	.5	5
Public Speaking (JSRCC)	B	.5	4*
Government and Politics	A	.5	4
French II (JSRCC)	A	1	5*
Art History	A	1	5*
CSC 202 Comp. Sci. (JSRCC)	B	.5	4*
Semester Total		4	27
Cumulative Total		27	184

Cumulative GPA 4.08

Basic Information

Grading Scale:
A—Superior (4)
B—Good (3)
C—Average (2)
D—Below Average (1)
P—Pass (0)
F—Fail (0)
*—Weighted Points

Unit Standard:
One unit represents 120 hours of guided study per 36-week school year.

Abbreviations:
Credit by Examination (AP) or (CLEP) follows Course Description. Grade assigned is based upon percentile ranking of test results, as well as class work, and weighted grade points are granted.

Dual-Credit Courses:
(JSRCC) follows Course Description. Grade and course descriptions issued by J. Sargeant Reynolds Community College. Only high-school-level credit is recorded on this transcript. Weighted grade points are granted for college courses.

Awards & Achievements:

Certification of Official Transcript

Select both lines of text and align flush right, as shown in the sample.

4. In the first cell beneath "High School Transcript," type "School:" Next, grab the right border of this cell and drag to the left until you reach "School:" and cannot go any farther. Tab to the next cell and enter the name of the school; then hit return and type the address as shown.

5. Tab to the fourth cell and type "Course Description." Continue tabbing and entering column headings in each cell in this row to match the text in the sample table. Choose Arial 10 point, bold italic for your font style.

6. Next go to the fifth cell under "School." Highlight it and the cell next to it. Go to the Table menu and select "Merge Cells." Type "Basic Information" in the newly merged cell.

7. Click in the cell below "Basic Information" and highlight it, the cell next to it, and all of the cells below them except for the last two. Go to the Table menu and select "Merge Cells."

8. Enter the headings as shown in the newly merged cell under "Basic Information" as in the table shown, using Arial 9 point, bold italic. Add and delete headings as necessary to match your needs. When you later enter text under the headings, use Arial 8 point in regular font.

9. Click in the last cell in this column and highlight it and the cell next to it. Go to the Table menu and select "Merge Cells." Type "Certifying Signature" in Arial 9 point.

10. Now place cursor next to "School." Go to the Table menu and choose "Split Table," which will divide your table into two parts. Select the top table, and go to "Table AutoFormat" in the Table menu. The first format option should be "(none)." Select this, and your table will have no visible borders, as you see in the sample.

11. Select and drag the right edge of the bottom table to align it with the top table, then size the columns to match the sample you have chosen, beginning with the column at the far right. You'll notice that as you size the columns, the words in the header column will stack. This will help fit them to the narrower column. Just don't make the column so narrow that the individual words split into pieces!

12. Select the entire second table and in "Table AutoFormat," choose "(none)," then in the Type menu of the Borders palette, choose the option that shows a border

around the edge of the selected area.

13. Select the header row, and in the Type menu of the Borders palette, choose the option that shows an inside horizontal border.

14. Finally, highlight all the remaining cells (the Course Description section) and choose Times New Roman or Arial 8 to 10 point font. You may use the largest font size that keeps the tables all on one page.

15. Remember that you may adjust font sizes and styles, borders, and column widths as necessary to accommodate your preferences. If you find that you need more than one page to enter all the information, simply insert a page break and copy and paste the table onto a second page. If you do so, you may wish to add page numbers in the footers to indicate page 1 of 2, page 2 of 2, etc.

Samples 2 and 3: Vertical Transcript Formats

The vertical transcripts can be organized by semester (page 80) or by subject (page 81). This basic format is created with two simple tables, making it easy to enter information by tabbing between cells.

Remember that you may adjust font sizes, styles, borders, and column widths as necessary to suit your needs. If, for some reason, you need more than one page to enter all the information, simply insert a page break from the Format menu, then copy and paste the table onto a second page. If you do so, you may wish to add page numbers in the footers to indicate page 1 of 2, page 2 of 2, etc.

Here is how you can create either transcript design in a word-processing program:

Create and Set Up Document

1. From the File menu, select "New" to create a blank document for the transcript.

2. Go back to the File menu and choose "Page Setup." Set all margins to 0.5". Ignore your program if it tells you these are outside the printable area, because they usually are not.

3. Save your document, giving it a descriptive file name such as the student's initials followed by "transcript."

4. Go to the Table menu and activate "Show Gridlines." (If the menu says "Hide

Gridlines," simply click on it so that it says "Show Gridlines" instead.) This will enable you to see all the table lines as you work, but the grid will not print. When you finish creating the transcript, you can hide the gridlines and see what it will look like when it's printed.

Create Table I for the Identity Section

1. Choose "Insert Table" from the Table menu and create a table with 4 columns and 6 rows. Select "Autofit to Contents" and click "OK."

2. Highlight ("Select") the first row of the table. Go to the Table menu and select "Merge Cells." Type "High School Transcript" and center it in the merged cell.

3. In the first cell of the second row, type "School:" In the third cell in the second row, type "Student:"

4. Now grab the right border of the table, (i.e., place the cursor on the border until you see two parallel bars with arrows pointing right and left), then click and drag to the right margin and release.

5. Grab the right edge of the cell with "Student" and drag to the right past "Transcript" above, about an inch from the edge of the table. Then grab the left edge of the cell with "Student" and drag to the right until the word "Student" lines up underneath "Transcript" above.

6. Grab the right edge of the cell with "Student" again and drag left until it stops and won't go any further. Select the entire table and format the text to Arial 11 point bold.

7. Select the entire table, and go to "Table AutoFormat" in the Table menu. The first format option should be "None." Select this and your table will have no visible borders, as you see in the sample.

8. The Identity Section is now ready for you to enter information. You will type information about the school in column 2, and about the student in column 4.

Create Table II for Basic Information and Course Record

1. With your cursor positioned outside the first table, hit return and insert a new table

with 7 columns and 10 rows. Select "Autofit to Contents" and click "OK."

2. Select the entire table and in "Table AutoFormat" select "Classic 1," or a similar format that sets off only the header row and first column.

3. Place cursor in the first cell of the first row and type "Basic Information." Tab across the first row, typing in headings for the format you have chosen. Highlight the entire row and format text to Arial 10 point bold italic.

4. Select and drag the right edge of the table to align it with the first table, then size the columns to match the sample you have chosen, beginning with the column at the far right. You'll notice that as you size the columns, the words in the header column will stack. This will help fit them to the narrower column. Just don't make the column so narrow that the individual words split into pieces!

5. Place cursor in the first column under "Basic Information" and select all cells in the column except for the last one. From the Table menu, choose "Merge Cells."

6. Enter the headings as shown under "Basic Information," using Arial 9 point bold italic. Add or delete headings to fit your needs. When you return later to fill in text under the headings, use Arial 8 point regular.

7. In the last cell of this column, type "Certifying Signature" in Arial 9 point regular. Use the line tool in the drawing palette (you will find this under "Toolbars" in the View menu) to draw a line right above the words. This is where you will sign the completed transcript.

8. Now highlight all the remaining cells (the Course Description section) and choose Times New Roman or Arial 8 to 10 point. You may use the largest font size that keeps the tables all on one page.

There! Now you can fill in all the course information. The table will grow to fit, and you'll end up with a very sharp-looking transcript. Wasn't that easy?

High School Transcript

School: Bandini High School
1913 Honey Run Road
Sites, CA 90000
888-123-4567
www.EverydayEducation.com

Student: Olivia Tate Shearin
Date of Birth: 3/19/2001
Gender: Female
Admission Date: 08/2014
Graduation Date: 12/2017

Basic Information	Term	Course Description	Grade	Units Earned	Grade Points	GPA
Grading Scale: A—Superior (4) B—Good (3) C—Average (2) D—Below Average (1) P—Pass (0) F—Fail (0) *—Weighted Points	Fall 2014	English I: Literature & Composition	A	.5	4	
		Algebra 1/2	B	.5	3	
		American History	A	.5	4	
		Earth Science	A	.5	4	
		Physical Education: Volleyball	B	.5	0	
		Choir: Mixed Chorus	A	.5	4	
		Semester Total		3	19	3.8
Unit Standard: One unit represents 120 hours of guided study per 36-week school year.	Spring 2015	English I: Literature & Composition	A	.5	4	
		Algebra 1/2	B	.5	3	
		American History	A	.5	4	
		Earth Science	A	.5	4	
		Physical Education: Softball	A	.5	0	
Abbreviations: **Credit by Examination** (AP) or (CLEP) follows Course Description. Grade assigned is based upon percentile ranking of test results, as well as class work, and weighted grade points are granted.		Art History and Appreciation	A	.5	4	
		Semester Total		3	19	3.8
		Cumulative Total		6	38	
	Fall 2015	English II: American Literature	A	.5	4	
		Algebra I	B	.5	3	
		Western Civilization I	B	.5	4*	
		Biology I	A	.5	4	
		Physical Education: Swimming	B	.5	0	
		CSC 155 Computer Concepts and Applications (JSRCC)	B	1	8*	
		Semester Total		3.5	24	3.8
Dual-Credit Courses: (JSRCC) follows Course Description. Grade and course descriptions issued by Maxwell-Chico Community College. Only high-school-level credit is recorded on this transcript. Weighted grade points are granted for college courses.	Spring 2016	English II: American Literature	A	.5	4	
		Algebra I	B	.5	3	
		Western Civilization I (CLEP)	A	.5	5*	
		Biology I	A	.5	4	
		Physical Education: Soccer	B	.5	0	
		Choir: Mixed and Men's Chorus	A	.5	4	
		Semester Total		3	20	4.0
		Cumulative Total		12.5	82	
Awards & Achievements:	Fall 2016	English III: British Literature	A	.5	4	
		Algebra II	B	.5	3	
		Western Civilization II	A	.5	5*	
		Chemistry I	A	.5	4	
		Physical Education: Football	B	.5	0	
		Choir: Quartet Arrangements	A	.5	4	
		Semester Total		3	20	4.0
	Spring 2017	English III: British Literature	A	.5	4	
		Algebra II	B	.5	3	
		Western Civilization II (CLEP)	A	.5	5*	
		Chemistry I	A	.5	4	
		Physical Education: Horseback Riding	B	.5	0	
		Applied Music: Individual Vocal Instruction	A	.5	4	
		Semester Total		3	20	4.0
		Cumulative Total		18.5	122	
	Fall 2017	English IV: World Literature	A	.5	4	
		Analysis and Interpretation of Literature (CLEP)	A	1	10*	
		MTH 166 Pre-Calculus With Trigonometry (JSRCC)	C	1	6*	
		Government and Politics (CLEP)	A	.5	5*	
		PHY 121 Principles of Physics (JSRCC)	B	1	8*	
		Applied Music: Piano	B	.5	3	
Certifying Signature		Semester Total		4.5	37	4.22
		Cumulative Total		23	159	3.96

Sample Transcripts and Diploma

High School Transcript

School: Walnut Creek High School
1913 Honey Run Road
Walnut Creek, Ohio, 40000
888-123-4567
www.EverydayEducation.com

Student: Sebastian Cabot
Date of Birth: 3/19/2001
1808 Indian Tree Trail
Walnut Creek, Ohio, 40000
GPA: Graduation Date: 12/2017

Basic Information	Course Description by Subject	Grade Sem. 1	Grade Sem. 2	Units Earned	GPA Points
Grading Scale: A—Superior (4) B—Good (3) C—Average (2) D—Below Average (1) P—Pass (0) F—Fail (0) *—Weighted Points	English I: Introduction to Literature	A	A	1	8
	English II: Literature & Composition - Honors	A	A	1	9
	English III: American Literature - CLEP	A	A	1	10
	English IV: British Literature - CLEP	A	A	1	10
	Introduction to Journalism	A		.5	4
Unit Standard: One unit represents 120 hours of guided study per 36-week school year.	Creative Writing	A		.5	4
	U.S. History - Early Colonization to 1877 - CLEP	A		1	5
Abbreviations: **Credit by Examination**(AP) or (CLEP) follows Course Description. Grade assigned is based upon percentile ranking of test results, as well as class work, and weighted grade points are granted.	American History: 1865 to Present – CLEP	B		1	4
	U.S. Government and Politics - AP	B		1	4
	Western Civ. I - Ancient Near East to 1648 - CLEP	A	A	1	10
Dual-Credit Courses: (WC) follows Course Description. Grade and course descriptions issued by Wayne College. Only high-school-level credit is recorded on this transcript. Weighted grade points are granted for college courses.	Western Civ. II - 1648 to Present	A	A	1	10
	European History - AP	A		1	5
	Human Geography - AP	B		1	4
Awards & Achievements:	Algebra I	B	C	1	5
	Algebra II	C	C	1	4
	Geometry	A	B	1	7
	French I	A	A	1	8
	French II	A	A	1	8
	French Literature - AP	A	B	1	9
	Biology	B	B	1	6
	Chemistry - JSRCC	C	C	1	6
Certifying Signature					

Sample 4: Check-Off Transcript

This is a super-simple transcript model. If you're in a hurry, or you haven't kept grade records, simply check off classes taken, sign the certification line, and you're done.

Because this form is pretty self-explanatory, I didn't fill out a sample. You can see the blank form on page 111. As classes are completed, you can write a letter grade in the column under the appropriate year. If you don't provide grades, just check off each class as it is completed. Simple! As with each of the other samples, you may use your own title, use parents' names in place of the school name, even change subject headings to customize it as you please.

1. Open a new document and set your margins at 0.5".

2. From the Table menu in your word processor, insert a table, with 50 rows and 7 columns. Set it to "Autofit to Contents" so that you can adjust the column widths to match the sample.

3. Select the entire first row of the table, go to the Table menu, and click on "Merge Cells."

4. Type in the document heading using Arial 18 point, centered.

5. In the second row of the table, merge the first three cells and the second four cells, leaving two cells in which you will type the Identity Information.

6. Type the table headings in 10 or 12 point in row 3 of the table, and the subject list in about 8 point in the first column on the left, as shown in the sample on page 111. You may customize the subject list as you prefer.

7. In the second row from the bottom, merge the first three cells and the second four cells, leaving two cells in which you will type the Basic Information.

8. Select the last row of the table, merge the cells, and type in the certification line.

Alternatives to Doing It Yourself

If, after you know what to do and how to do it, you still don't want to create a transcript, there are some alternatives. You may want to:

- Have your student enroll in a community college, then transfer to a four-year university

- Assign transcript creation to your student as part of a class in Business Documents or Computer Competence

- Barter with an experienced homeschooler or competent friend for transcript services

- Hire someone else who can do the job. (Give them this book, and they'll know just what to do!)

I encourage you to choose the option that is best for your family and not to be intimidated by the transcript process. It really isn't hard!

Community College/Dual Credit

Most community colleges and even a few four-year universities accept teens as dual-credit students without a transcript. You can enroll your student for a semester or two, then have him or her apply to the four-year university as a transfer student. If he has 24 credits or more from the community college, most four-year schools will not require a transcript.

For our 16-year-old son, Craig, the application process was simple. We filled out the application form found in the community college's semester course listing and mailed it in. Because placement tests were required for English and mathematics, he went in and took those on campus. When registration opened, I called the registration office, asked for the dual-credit counselor, and inquired if there were any special forms to fill out for homeschooled dual-credit students. There were none, and based upon Craig's SAT and placement test scores, the counselor approved the four courses Craig needed to take. After that, it was just a matter of registering and paying. No transcript required! Many home-schoolers have followed this route and found it a very simple path to college. If you'd like to do it, here's a checklist:

- Select a convenient community college
- Pick up a course guide or access it online
- Fill out and mail the application for admission
- Apply for financial aid if your student will attend full-time

- Have student schedule and take required placement tests (usually language arts and math)

- Contact dual-credit counselor (if any) to clear course choices

- Register and pay for first semester

- Buy books (online sources can be cheaper than the student bookstore—see links on my website, www.Everyday-Education.com)

- Tell your student to go to class, learn new study habits, pass courses!

- Register student for the next semester

When your student is ready to declare a major, he should visit the student services office (it's not always called that, but it is the office that handles registration and enrollment) and change his student status from non-curricular to curricular (degree-seeking).

Your state's community college rules may not permit students under 18 to declare a major without a GED or high-school diploma, in which case you can choose to have your student take the GED (a very easy exam), issue your own diploma, or transfer him to a more flexible school. Private college are usually more flexible than state schools.

Student-Created Transcript

If you're not ready to let your student head off to college just yet but are not comfortable with creating the transcript, assign it to your student, perhaps as part of an Introduction to Computers or Introduction to Business Documents class. Learning to create not only a transcript but also a resume and business forms of all types, the student would be better prepared for the business world and a possible future role as a homeschool parent.

Barter Services or Hire Someone

In most city phone directories, under "Administrative Services," "Typing," or "Secretarial Services," you can find someone to type up the transcript for you. Or perhaps someone in your local support group would be willing to do so. Just remember that you must have all the information ready, because the person you hire won't be able to run around looking for missing pieces of information, and they may not even realize when something is missing.

The bottom line is that creating a transcript and diploma is a pretty straightforward process once you understand its purpose, its audience, and the practical basics of grading and granting credit. Whether you do it yourself or get someone else to do it for you, you'll end up with a transcript that works.

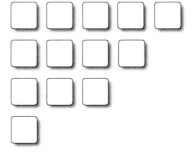

Glossary

AP – See "Advanced Placement."

Accommodations – Special conditions permitted so that students with a disability will be able to complete fairly.

Advanced Placement – The earned privilege of skipping entry-level college course in favor of more advanced study.

Carnegie unit – This is the name for the kind of credit that is awarded in high school. It equals about 120 hours of guided instruction.

CLEP – College Level Examination Program – A group of standardized tests designed to measure subject-area knowledge for the purpose of granting college credit.

Community College – A two-year college, granting associate's degrees.

Credit – Acknowledgement of a student's completion of a specific course of study. Also see "Carnegie unit."

Credit-by-Exam – College credit earned by taking a standardized test.

DSST – A group of standardized, college-level exams, formerly known as DANTES.

DOE – See "Department of Education."

Department of Education – A branch of the government dedicated to regulating education in the United States.

Diploma – A ceremonial document certifying that the recipient has completed high school.

Dual Credit – Classes taken for both high-school and college credit.

GED – General Equivalency Diploma. This exam is often taken by people who have dropped out of high school. It signifies that the student has achieved at least eighth-grade competence in basic academic subjects. I don't recommend it unless you absolutely have to have it to get into a college.

GPA – See "Grade Point Average."

Grade Points – See "Quality Points."

Grade Point Average – The total score of a student's quality points, divided by the number of classes taken.

Grading Scale – A description of the standards used to define letter grades.

Graduation – A ceremony marking the completion of high-school requirements.

FAFSA – Free Application for Student Aid.

Financial Aid – Grants, loans, scholarships, and work study obtained from the government and from colleges and used to pay tuition.

HSLDA – Home School Legal Defense Association.

High-School Record Notebook – A notebook containing Subject Worksheets from *Transcripts Made Easy*, as well as other documents relevant to the student's high-school experience.

Homeschool Law – The group of statutes that define conditions for homeschooling in your state.

Honors – A designation that indicates a deliberately challenging class or course of study.

Glossary

IEP – Individualized Education Plan created by a public school for a specific public-school student with special needs.

Junior College – See "Community College."

Matriculate – To begin college classes.

Portfolio – An organized collection of student work with the purpose of requesting credit.

Quality Points – The numerical value assigned to letter grades in order to calculate a grade point average. Also known as grade points.

Quarter – An academic grading period of approximately ten weeks.

Reading Log – A record of reading done for academic assignments and for pleasure.

SAT – Scholastic Aptitude Test – An exam administered to high-school students, designed to test aptitude for higher-level learning.

SAT II – Subject-area exams for high-school students, designed to test knowledge in specific subject areas for the purpose of college admissions and/or advanced placement.

SEP – Student Education Plan, usually for students with special needs.

Secondary School – Grades 9–12.

Semester – An academic grading period of 14–18 weeks, usually half the school year.

Special Need – Any requirement for above-average academic assistance due to a physical or mental disability.

Subject Worksheet – A gathering place for raw information related to each subject studied in high school.

Transcript – A record of subjects studied and grades earned.

Unit – See "Carnegie Unit."

Weighted Grade Points – A grading system in which an extra whole or half grade point is awarded for advanced work.

Resources

Reference

Shorter Oxford English Dictionary – At the risk of igniting a new round of the dictionary war, I recommend this fascinating two-volume dictionary as the very best dictionary you can afford to buy (the unabridged version is even more wonderful, but it is over ten volumes and rather expensive). The beauty of this dictionary is the sample of word usage that accompanies almost every one of the definitions (over half a million definitions included!). Samples are taken from great literature, including the Bible, Shakespeare, and other great works. This makes dictionary browsing a newly pleasurable pastime, and helps place words and expressions in the context of literary history.

College textbooks – For standardized test preparation, reference for research papers, designing a scope and sequence for a unit study, and in-depth subject overview, it's hard to beat a college textbook. Both students and parents will find useful information there.

Inspiration

The 7 Habits of Highly Effective People, by Stephen Covey – One of the books that I wish everyone could read before making plans for life. Steven Covey's principles are extremely helpful.

What Color Is Your Parachute?, by Richard Nelson Bolles – A classic resource for discovering personal aptitudes and talents, with a focus on finding a suitable career. His website has good links and information (link to it from my website, www.Everyday-Education.com).

Hothouse Transplants, by Matt Duffy – Stories of homeschoolers who have graduated and are successful and happy in what they are doing. Quite helpful in calming parental fears.

Things We Wish We'd Known, edited by Bill and Diana Waring – Short essays from fifty veteran homeschoolers. Very helpful in determining priorities and defusing worries.

Preparing Sons to Provide for a Single-Income Family, by Steven Maxwell – An inspiring book available from Titus2.com.

The Ultimate Guide to Homeschooling, by Debra Bell – This regularly updated classic offers very solid information from an experienced homeschooler with high standards.

The Teenage Liberation Handbook, by Grace Llewellyn – This is an interesting and reassuring resource from an unschooling perspective. There is inappropriate language in some of the teen comments, but the body of the book can be quite helpful in defusing anxiety and finding interesting learning resources.

Dumbing Us Down, by John Taylor Gatto – This brief classic is a reminder of some of the reasons we want to homeschool through high school. A must-read!

Test-Related Resources

Most of these sites provide practice tests and complete information about the exams as well as online registration and links to other helpful information.

SAT I and II, AP, and CLEP: www.collegeboard.com

ACT: www.act.org

DSST: www.getcollegecredit.com

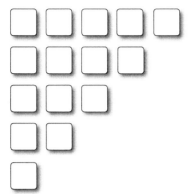

Reproducible Forms

Here are all the forms you will need to keep an impressive array of high-school records. Please don't feel that you must use them all. Use what you need, and feel free to adapt them to your own situation. You may keep them in perfect tidiness on your computer; you may keep them as a slapdash assortment in a three-ring-binder; or you may just go ahead and write in the book. The forms are yours to use within your family as you see fit. Enjoy!

Reading Log

Activities Log

Class Profile

Subject Worksheets

Blank Transcript Forms

Reading Log

Date	Author	Title	Rating	Comments

Activities Log

Date	Activity	Skills	Tools	Time	Comments

Class Profile

Class: Date:

Description:

Outside Resources/Tutors:

Final Grade/Comments:

Readings	Assignments

Grading:

©2007 Janice Campbell

Subject Worksheet: English

High School Units Required: State ____ College ___Other____ _____ _____

Units Earned: Grade 9 ____ _Grade_10 ____ Grade_11____ Grade 12 _____ _____

College Credits Earned: Total ____ By _Exam__ Class _____ _____

Units Earned	Course / Book	Date	Grade	Test Score	Comments
Includes English composition, literature (American, English, world, comparative, etc.), journalism, creative writing, business writing, poetry etc.					

Subject Worksheet: Mathematics

High School Units Required: State _____ College _____ Other _____

Units Earned: Grade 9 _____ Grade 10 _____ Grade 11 _____ Grade 12 _____

College Credits Earned: Total _____ By Exam _____ Class _____

Units Earned	Course / Book	Date	Grade	Test Score	Comments

Includes Algebra I & II, Geometry, Calculus, Trigonometry, etc. Some math classes such as "Consumer Math" are not college prep, but may be listed. You may use text book titles as course names.

Subject Worksheet: History

High School Units Required: State _____ College _____ Other _____

Units Earned: Grade 9 _____ Grade 10 _____ Grade 11 _____ Grade 12 _____

College Credits Earned: Total _____ By Exam _____ Class _____

Units Earned	Course / Book	Date	Grade	Test Score	Comments
Includes American history (at least one unit required), western civilization, European history, African studies, 20th century conflicts, ancient history, etc.					

©2007 Janice Campbell

Subject Worksheet: Natural Sciences

High School Units Required: State _____ College _____ Other _____

Units Earned: Grade 9 _____ Grade 10 _____ Grade 11 _____ Grade 12 _____

College Credits Earned: Total _____ By Exam _____ Class _____

Units Earned	Course / Book	Date	Grade	Test Score	Comments
Includes biology, chemistry, physics, and life sciences, as well as focused topics such as astronomy, anatomy, geology, ecology, archaeology, etc.					

Subject Worksheet: Social Sciences

High School Units Required: State _____ College _____ Other _____

Units Earned: Grade 9 _____ Grade 10 _____ Grade 11 _____ Grade 12 _____

College Credits Earned: Total _____ By Exam _____ Class _____

Units Earned	Course / Book	Date	Grade	Test Score	Comments

Includes law, cultural studies, linguistics, psychology, geography, sociology, anthropology, social policy, economics, political sciences, research methods, etc.

Subject Worksheet: Religion and Philosophy

High School Units Required: State _____ College _____ Other _____

Units Earned: Grade 9 _____ Grade 10 _____ Grade 11 _____ Grade 12 _____

College Credits Earned: Total _____ By Exam _____ Class _____

Units Earned	Course / Book	Date	Grade	Test Score	Comments
Includes Old and New Testament studies, worldview studies, comparative religions, introduction to philosophy, ethics, etc.					

Subject Worksheet: Foreign Language

High School Units Required: State _____ College _____ Other _____

Units Earned: Grade 9 _____ Grade 10 _____ Grade 11 _____ Grade 12 _____   _____

College Credits Earned: Total _____ By Exam _____ Class _____

Units Earned	Course / Book	Date	Grade	Test Score	Comments

Includes the study of any language other than the native tongue, including American Sign Language. High-school foreign language study should include grammar and writing, as well as speaking.

Subject Worksheet: Fine Arts

High School Units Required: State _____ College _____ Other _____

Units Earned: Grade 9 _____ Grade 10 _____ Grade 11 _____ Grade 12 _____

College Credits Earned: Total _____ By Exam _____ Class _____

Units Earned	Course / Book	Date	Grade	Test Score	Comments
Includes art history, art appreciation, music theory, music performance, drama, and applied arts, such as painting, sculpture, photography, and dance performance.					

©2007 Janice Campbell

Subject Worksheet: Practical Arts

High School Units Required: State _____ College _____ Other _____

Units Earned: Grade 9 _____ Grade 10 _____ Grade 11 _____ Grade 12 _____

College Credits Earned: Total _____ By Exam _____ Class _____

Units Earned	Course / Book	Date	Grade	Test Score	Comments

Includes driver education, home economics, sewing, woodworking, auto mechanics, computer skills, office skills and procedures, small engine repair, equine management, etc.

Subject Worksheet: Health/ Physical Education

High School Units Required: State _____ College _____ Other _____

Units Earned: Grade 9 _____ Grade 10 _____ Grade 11 _____ Grade 12 _____

College Credits Earned: Total _____ By Exam _____ Class _____

Units Earned	Course / Book	Date	Grade	Test Score	Comments
Health includes nutrition, fitness, lifestyle, and basic anatomy. Physical Education includes any fitness activity, such as swimming, skiing, bicycling, weight training, aerobics, yoga, or team sports.					

Subject Worksheet: Electives

High School Units Required: State _____ College _____ Other _____

Units Earned: Grade 9 _____ Grade 10 _____ Grade 11 _____ Grade 12 _____

College Credits Earned: Total _____ By Exam _____ Class _____

Units Earned	Course / Book	Date	Grade	Test Score	Comments
Includes any classes or activities that don't fit into other subject categories, such as public speaking, debate, entrepreneurship, volunteer activities, job-related activities, etc.					

Subject Worksheet

High School Units Required: State _____ College _____ Other _____

Units Earned: Grade 9 _____ Grade 10 _____ Grade 11 _____ Grade 12 _____

College Credits Earned: Total _____ By Exam _____ Class _____

Units Earned	Course / Book	Date	Grade	Test Score	Comments

Blank Transcript Forms

I would like to think that I've convinced you that it's not hard to create a transcript on the computer. However, if you are wedded to your typewriter and want to try filling in the transcript that way, here are blank copies of each of the forms. I don't really recommend doing it this way, as it is much harder than doing it on the computer, but if you really want to try it, you can.

You will need more than one page, if you type it, so there are a couple of things you need to do differently.

1. Include all three sections on each page.

2. Number the pages to show both the page number and the total number of pages. This way, if the pages get separated, the admissions department will know how many there are. The numbers should look like this: 1/3, 2/3, 3/3, and the number should be placed somewhere on the lower edge of the page.

3. Once you have it completed, you may want to consider having someone with computer experience re-create it on the computer.

The four blank forms include:

*   Horizontal Transcript

*   Vertical Transcript

*   Subject-Order Transcript

*   Check-Off Transcript

HIGH SCHOOL TRANSCRIPT

School:

Admission:
Graduation:

Basic Information

Course Description	Grade	Units Earned	Grade Points	Course Description	Grade	Units Earned	Grade Points

Certification of Official Transcript

©2007 Janice Campbell

High School Transcript

School:

Student:

Date of Birth:
Gender:
Admission Date:
Graduation Date:

Basic Information	Term	Course Description	Grade	Units Earned	Grade Points	GPA
Grading Scale: A—Superior (4) B—Good (3) C—Average (2) D—Below Average (1) P—Pass (0) F—Fail (0) *—Weighted Points **Unit Standard:** **Abbreviations:** **Awards & Achievements:** **Certifying Signature**						

High School Transcript

School: Name   **Student:**

Address   Date of Birth:

                                       Address:

Phone/e-mail   Phone/email

Student's Graduation Date   GPA: Graduation Date:

Basic Information	*Course Description by Subject*	*Grade Sem. 1*	*Grade Sem.2*	*Units Earned*	*GPA Points*
Grading Scale: A—Superior (4) B—Good (3) C—Average (2) D—Below Average (1) P—Pass (0) F—Fail (0) *—Weighted Points ***Unit Standard:*** ***Abbreviations:*** ***Awards & Achievements:*** ***Certifying Signature***					

©2007 Janice Campbell

High School Transcript

Subject Studied	Year 1	Year 2	Year 3	Year 4	Credits	Awards/Notes
English						
American Literature						
British Literature						
World Literature						
Latin						
French						
Spanish						
German						
U.S. History						
Western Civilization						
World History						
Civics / Government						
Pre-Algebra						
Algebra						
Geometry						
Calculus						
Trigonometry						
Physical Science						
Biology						
Chemistry						
Physics						
Environmental Science						
Old Testament						
New Testament						
Religion Elective						
Art History						
Studio Art						
Music Theory						
Music History / Appreciation						
Applied Music: Vocal						
Applied Music: Piano						
Applied Music: Instrumental						
Social Sciences						
Psychology: Family Life						
Social Science Elective						
Business Elective						
Computer Skills						
Computer Programming						
Web Design						
Graphic Arts						
Photography						
Physical Education						
Elective						
Elective						

School

Student

Grading Scale:

Abbreviations:

Certified by:

Contributors

Special-Needs Consultation

Judith B. Munday, M.A., M.Ed.

Educational Consultant

Virginia Licensed, Endorsed K–12 Learning Disabilities

www.hishelpinschool.com

College Counselor Contacts

Rob Bovey, Admissions Counselor

Jennifer Burke, Admissions Counselor

Corban College

800-845-3005, ext. 7008

www.corban.edu

Formerly Western Baptist College

Kim McCarty, Director of Admissions
Seton Hill University
www.setonhill.edu

Mark Lapreziosa, Assistant Vice President of Enrollment Management
Tamara Lapman, Enrollment Management Counselor
Arcadia University
450 South Easton Road
Glenside, PA 19038
215-572-4046
lapmant@arcadia.edu

Karen P. Condeni, Dean and Vice President of Enrollment
Ohio Northern University
Ada, Ohio 45810
www.onu.edu

James Townsend, Director of Admissions
LeTourneau University
jamestownsend@letu.edu

Kelly Stoner, Admissions Counselor/International Student Recruiter
E-mail: kstoner@wilson.edu
717-262-2002

Jeffrey C. Mincey, Director of Admissions
Grove City College
100 Campus Drive
Grove City, PA 16127
724-458-2100

Jolane Rohr, Director of Admissions
Manchester College
www.manchester.edu

Contributors

Monica Inzer, Dean of Admission and Financial Aid
Hamilton College
www.hamilton.edu

Nancy Davidson, Dean of Admission
Augustana College
2001 South Summit Avenue
Sioux Falls, SD 57197
800-727-2844
www.augie.edu

Sam Smith
Stonehill College
www.stonehill.edu

Moishe B. Singer, MPH, Assistant Director of Admissions
Yeshiva University
500 West 185th Street – F419
New York, NY 10033
www.yu.edu
singer@yu.edu
212-960-5277

Transcripts Made Easy

Text is Adobe Garamond.

Headers are Kabel Demi.

Tables and charts are Arial and Helvetica.

Also used are Dakota and Lucida Blackletter.

Copyediting and layout by WordsRight

Richmond, VA

sbs@WordsRight.net

Cover design by

Communication Graphics

Richmond, VA

bob.sheppard3@verizon.net

Index

About the Author

Janice Campbell is a lifelong learner, writer, and conference speaker who has enjoyed homeschooling since the late 1980s. She and her husband, Donald, were blessed by the privilege of home educating their four sons, and watching them graduate early and get a jump start on college and on life. Janice takes joy in sharing with others what she has learned, and she offers workshops on writing, teaching literature, and on homeschooling through high school, including early college and entrepreneurship.

Janice graduated *cum laude* from Mary Baldwin College with a B.A. in English. She is author of *Excellence in Literature: Reading and Writing Through the Classics,* a literature curriculum for grades 8-12; *Transcripts Made Easy*; and *Get a Jump Start on College!*; editor of *The Virginia Homeschool Manual*; and creator of the Beat-the-Clock Essay Workshop™, an innovative one-day workshop that prepares students for timed SAT, CLEP, and ACT essays. Janice blogs at www.Janice-Campbell.com and her website, www.Everyday-Education.com, offers information, resources, inspiration, and a free e-newsletter.

Order Form

Dear Friends,

Most of these resources are available online at www.Everyday-Education.com, and that's the easiest way to order. If I can answer any questions, please feel free to e-mail me at jceved@comcast.net. Order forms with payment by check or money order may be mailed to: Everyday Education, LLC, P.O. Box 549, Ashland, VA 23005-3150.

Sincerely,

Janice Campbell

Quantity	Item Description	Each	Total
Excellence in Literature			
	English I: Introduction to Literature	29.00	
	English II: Literature and Composition	29.00	
	English III: American Literature	29.00	
	English IV: British Literature	29.00	
	English V: World Literature	29.00	
Help for Homeschooling Through High School... and Beyond			
	Transcripts Made Easy	25.00	
	Get a Jump Start on College! A Practical Guide for Teens	18.00	
	Conquer the Test SAT Prep - 3 Audio CDs plus Handbook	49.00	
Audio CDs			
	Homeschooling Through High School		
	Teaching Language Arts the Easy, Natural Way		
	How to Evaluate Writing		
	Paying for College		
	Microbusiness		
	Making Time for Things That Matter		
	Caring for Our Own		
	Subtotal		
	Tax (5% for VA residents only)		
	Shipping	4.95	
	Order Total		

Ship to: **Name** _____

Address _____

City/State/ZIP _____